FORMS OF EXILE IN JEWISH LITERATURE AND THOUGHT

Twentieth-Century Central Europe and Movement to America

An electronic version of this book is freely available, thanks to the support of libraries working with Knowledge Unlatched. KU is a collaborative initiative designed to make high quality books Open Access for the public good. The Open Access ISBN for this book is 978-1-64469-406-0. More information about the initiative and links to the Open Access version can be found at www.knowledgeunlatched.org.

FORMS OF EXILE IN JEWISH LITERATURE AND THOUGHT

Twentieth-Century Central Europe and Movement to America

BRONISLAVA VOLKOVÁ

BOSTON
2021

Library of Congress Cataloging-in-Publication Data:
A catalog record for this book as available from the Library of Congress.

ISBN 9781644695906 (paperback)
ISBN 9781644694060 (open access PDF)
ISBN 9781644694077 (ePub)

On the cover: "Talking Stones," by Bronislava Volková. Collage.
Cover design by Ivan Grave.
Book design by Tatiana Vernikov.

Published by Academic Studies Press
1577 Beacon Street
Brookline, MA 02446, USA

press@academicstudiespress.com
www.academicstudiespress.com

Contents

Acknowledgements

The publication of this book was possible thanks to a grant from the Robert A. and Sandra S. Borns Jewish Studies Program, at Indiana University.

The book was also selected by the Knowledge Unlatched Selection Committee 2020 (comprised of specialist subject librarians from all over the world) to be part of the "KU Select Books Collection 2020, Humanities and Social Science" as one of 343 titles worldwide selected for Open Access release.

Behind the city! Understand? Behind!
Outside! Across the dam!
Life here is a place where it's impossible to live.
A Jewish quarter . . .

Thus is it not a hundred times better
to become an Eternal Jew?
Because for everyone who is not a swine,
a Jewish pogrom stews.

Life. It's alive only through renegades!
Through the Judases of the faiths!
Onto Solomon's islands!
To hell! To anywhere but

to life, which suffers only renegades, only
sheep for the executioner!
I trample the certificate permitting my right to live
with my feet!

I tread it down! For David's shield!
Into the compost of the bodies!
Isn't it intoxicating that a Yid
did not want to live?!

A ghetto of chosen gatherings! Dam and ditch.
Do not seek indulgence!
In this most Christian of worlds
poets are treated as Yids!

—*Marina Tsvetaeva:*
Poem of the End, part 12, stanzas 7–12.
Translated by Bronislava Volková

Modern Western culture is in large part the work of exiles, émigrés, refugees. In the United States, academic, intellectual and aesthetic thought is what it is today because of refugees from fascism, communism, and other regimes given to the oppression and expulsion of dissidents.

And while it is true that literature and history contain heroic, romantic, glorious, even triumphant episodes in an exile's life, these are no more than efforts meant to overcome the crippling sorrow of estrangement.

—Edward Said:
Reflections on Exile

It seems proper that those who create art in a civilization of quasi-barbarism, which has made so many homeless, should themselves be poets unhoused and wanderers across language. Eccentric, aloof, nostalgic, deliberately untimely . . .

—George Steiner

[I]t is part of morality not to be at home in one's home.
—Theodor Adorno

The person who finds his homeland sweet is a tender beginner; he to whom every soil is as his native one is already strong; but he is perfect to whom the entire world is as a foreign place. The tender soul has fixed his love on one spot in the world; the strong person has extended his love to all places; the perfect man has extinguished his.

—Hugh of St. Victor
(twelfth-century theologian)

Introduction
A General History of Concepts of Exile

Exile is a very complex concept: it is multifaceted and has numerous implications. I have written about it in a personal way[1] in the past and I have also taught a class at Indiana University on this topic drawing on the unusually rich and interesting Jewish (predominantly German-language) twentieth-century writing of Central Europe. Ideas developed during these classes have served as a starting point for the present study.

Exile has generated wonderful writing since times immemorial — Sappho, Dante, Comenius, Zola, Mann, Joyce, Beckett, Solzhenitsyn, Conrad, to name a few outstanding examples). Twentieth-century European literature, however, plays a special role in the exploration of exile, due to the displacement of vast numbers of people caused by the brutal totalitarian regimes that took over many countries for extended periods of time, the increasing ease of traveling great distances, and technological progress.

This study is primarily focused on the variety of meanings that the term "exile" can take on and the different angles from which it can be examined. It is a study that looks at the inner meanings of exile, the types of inner withdrawal due to a lack of acceptance

---

[1] See Bronislava Volková, "Exil vnitřní a vnější," *Listopad* (2004): 12–19; "Exile: Inside and Out," in *The Writer Uprooted: Contemporary Jewish Exile Literature*, ed. Alvin Rosenfeld (Bloomington: Indiana UP, 2008), 161–176; "Psychological, Cultural, Historical and Spiritual Aspects of Exile," *Comenius, Journal of Euro-American Civilisation* 1, no. 2 (2014), 199–212; "Exil: psychologický, kulturně-historický, duchovní," *Český Dialog*, May 2015, http://www.cesky-dialog.net/clanek/6774-exil-psychologicky-kulturne-historicky-a-duchovni/.

by society of the intrinsic values of an individual, considering both the physical movement of a writer to another country and the background of such movement. Many kinds of authors from a number of different countries found themselves outcasts in exile, and their work (especially the protagonists in their writing) reflects this. Some of them committed suicide due to the harshness of their social situation and the impossibility of adapting to a new and foreign social environment. However, many contributed vastly different literary forms and created a large variety of thought patterns which all have a common thread.

The first part of the study deals with early twentieth-century issues and movement, while the second is focused on the Holocaust and beyond. I give the Jews a major role in this study for two reasons: 1) they had enormous cultural influence and were, in effect, the glue of Central European literature and thought; and 2) their long tradition of diasporic life and extraordinary persecution in the twentieth century arguably makes them the very embodiment of exile. Twentieth-century Europe was clearly characterized by the movement of nations due to the horrendously oppressive regimes which destroyed the natural life fiber of the existing societies— and the Jews became the first and most prominent victims of this phenomenon.

In the course of studying the issue of exile, the breadth of this concept and the multiple implications it takes on led me to identify what I call the *forms* of exile.

Exile, in the most basic sense, means to be away from one's home country, while either explicitly being refused permission to return or being threatened with imprisonment or death upon return. It is a type of punishment closely associated with solitude and isolation. Sometimes it involves a whole nation or large group, which makes up a so-called diaspora (a society within another nation, but away from its own); at other times it may simply concern individuals living in foreign environments.

Jews have been probably in the longest exile of this type (since 587 BCE; since 70 CE; after the rise of Islam in the seventh century; and again during the Crusades in the eleventh–thirteenth centuries). They fled to Western Europe, but were expelled from many countries there, only to be readmitted on payment to the local powers or governments later. From the Middle Ages onwards, they settled in large numbers in Eastern Europe, especially in Poland at the invitation of Casimir the Great in 1343; but their general situation improved only after the French Revolution when they were granted human rights. Meanwhile, mob violence was perpetrated against them in many countries. Pogroms were frequent in Eastern and Central Europe and culminated in the Nazi Holocaust, or the Shoah, of the 1940s. Jews fared best on the whole in the Anglophone countries during this period, where they were able to achieve at times considerable status. However, a day after the State of Israel was recognized by the UN in 1948, the Arab-Israeli War began.

The theme of exile appears already in Greek tragedy. It is closely connected with ostracism (Greek: *ostrakismos*), which was a procedure in the city-state of Athens in which any citizen could be expelled for ten years. While in some instances clearly expressed popular anger at the citizen was the reason, ostracism was often used preemptively. It was employed as a way of neutralizing someone thought to be a threat to the state or a potential tyrant. In general, the most common form of ostracism is refusing to communicate with a person. This, too, can take many forms. Refused communication, a person is effectively ignored and excluded from a given community. Such is the fate of both internal and external exiles.

This refusal of communication is an essential part of being an exile. Exile in a general sense means that an individual is not simply physically displaced, but is avoided or ostracized, due to not fitting into the prevalent moral and social values of their society of origin. In both cases social exclusion is what follows. This exclusion, like marginalization, can affect a writer's particular themes, as well as their artistic decisions. Exile can result not just from being a member of a particular social or gender group, then, but also from adhering to certain aesthetics.

Internal exile is also a kind of withdrawal. The withdrawn author often depicts, with great acuity, the most significant, albeit hidden, diseases of society, as well as finding new perspectives. The author is often harshly criticized, sometimes forbidden to publish altogether or, in less oppressive societies, simply ignored. This has an equally, if not more, detrimental effect. When writers are persecuted, they often become regarded as heros, someone with whom an oppressed nation can identify when it has no other recourse; and thus, paradoxically, such a writer may become central to the culture. In less oppressive regimes, however, the ostracized writer is left to his own devices and simply marginalized.

In her article on Shklovsky and Brodsky, Svetlana Boym, however, points out that exile can also be seen as a form of estrangement.[2] Leo Spitzer adds another shade of meaning to the word "exile," when he recalls his childhood and the society he was a part of when in exile in Bolivia—namely nostalgia mixed with critical memory, that is, looking at the past critically, yet with a certain longing at the same time. He also speaks of the layered identities of people combining their culture of origin with that of their new adopted home.[3]

Physical exile implies a veritable loss: of country, birthplace, language, support, and belonging, and in all cases an absence of an engaged and responsive community and thus most importantly a loss of meaning and communication. Meaning and communication can be recovered in many cases or recreated in roundabout ways, but a sense of natural bonds has forever been destroyed. These bonds, however, I believe, are replaced by a heightened capacity for transformation.

We find a radical lack of setting or strong depiction of place (of birth, life, or death) most pronouncedly in such writers as Peter Weiss, Nelly Sachs, and Paul Celan. I can strongly identify with this, as the same phenomenon is an element in my own poetry—it is situated most often nowhere and everywhere simultaneously. This interstitial quality makes such writing both more universal and more abstract.

---

[2]   Svetlana Boym, "Estrangement as a Lifestyle: Shklovsky and Brodsky," in *Exile and Creativity: Signposts, Travelers, Outsiders, Backward Glances*, ed. Susan Rubin Suleiman (Durham: Duke UP, 1998), 241–262.

[3]   Leo Spitzer "Persistent Memory," in Rubin Suleiman, *Exile and Creativity*, 384.

Exile leads to unusual productivity and original insights, which are often not readily received by the addressees of such writing, who generally view exiles as outsiders and often are unable to relate to their way of thinking. Exiles, in turn, typically create their own community based on the commonality of exclusion or persecution, not on intrinsic and cohesive closeness and shared interests of a primary kind. Their communal structures are tentative and vulnerable, usually highly temporary and typically an acute sense of isolation and loneliness is common to exiled authors.

This absence of a cohesive community, nevertheless, brings another inner transformation within the writer's psyche: they see through the illusions of communities often built on the bases of certain ideologies, nationalities, customs, blood bonds, and so on. As Hatja Garloff observes when she considers the post-Holocaust existence of Jews, an irredeemable dispersion is the very foundation of a diasporic community.[4]

I would argue that this kind of definition of community implies in itself that a community as such is fundamentally based on the idea of the nation; however, the idea of nation is frequently very destructive and superficial too. Richard Königsberg notes the illusionary character of history and the perverse and absurd rights that nations assume.[5] That said, what exiles lack in their community of origin, they can redeem in their potential openness toward a universal one. This gives them a tremendous freedom and breadth in their understanding of the world.

Leo Spitzer remarks that "desperate feelings of possible doom over trifles" is common among Holocaust survivors.[6] Some feel they made a lucky choice which led to their survival, others, as described in Marianne Hirsch's paper, feel forever tied in their minds to the past of their parents' world. Such a person may feel they they have never

---

[4] Hatja Garloff, *Words from Abroad*: *Trauma and Displacement in Postwar German Jewish Writers* (Detroit: Wayne State UP, 2005), 4.

[5] See Richard Königsberg, *The Nations Have the Right to Kill* (New York: Library of Social Science, 2014).

[6] Spitzer, "Persistent Memory," 384.

even experienced themselves, as their self was destroyed forever. This is a well-known characteristic of how the so-called "children of the Holocaust" perceive the world. Succumbing to desperate feelings over the trifles of daily life is a natural consequence of passing through experiences in life deemed as catastrophic trauma. They are a part of the post-traumatic psychological attitude.

Here, memory is also an act of mourning filled with rage and despair. This memory and distance from a world destroyed and unknowable persists in the second generation, so called children of the Holocaust. Hirsch calls this memory "postmemory," namely a memory formed not by recollection, but by imaginative investment and creation. "Postmemory characterizes the experience of those who grow up dominated by narratives that preceded their birth, whose own belated stories are displaced by the stories of the previous generation, shaped by traumatic events that can be neither fully understood nor re-created."[7]

The children of exiled Holocaust survivors can never return "home," they remain forever marginal or exiled, as the cities to which they can return are no longer those in which their parents had lived as Jews before the genocide, but are instead the cities where the genocide happened and from which they and their memory have been expelled. The postwar generation thus lives in a void, an exile from identity, time, and space, orphaned from a world they never knew.

Having lived in Communist Czechoslovakia, I can testify that there is another layer to this condition of post-memory, namely the sense of a lost world in a more general meaning of that word, a nostalgia for a world forever destroyed to us and never to be recovered or repaired. A double void of inner exile is thus present in the children growing up within their family's country of origin with the stories they have heard from their parents, or grandparents, about what life was like before it was snatched away by a totalitarian power.

---

[7] See Marianne Hirsch, "Past Lives," in Rubin Suleiman, *Exile and Creativity*, 418–421.

Edward Said argues that

> [t]he exile exists in a median state. Neither completely at one with the new setting nor fully disencumbered of the old, beset with half-involvements and half-detachments, nostalgic and sentimental on one level, an adept mimic or a secret outcast on another. Survival becomes the main imperative, and danger of getting too comfortable and secure constituting a threat that is constantly to be guarded against.[8]

The exiled person also always perceives things through comparison, from a double perspective, never in isolation (60). Furthermore, they often move away from centralizing authorities towards the margins, where they see things that are usually lost on people that have never traveled beyond the conventional and the comfortable (63).

Much literature concerning Central European territory, most notably interwar Czechoslovakia, has been devoted to German Jews, who had an important role as cultural mediators. They helped to bring important Czech writers and musicians into German cultural space via translations and popularizations. The best known was Max Brod, who was responsible for the world renown of Leoš Janáček, Jaromír Weinberger, Vítězslav Novák, Jaroslav Hašek, and Otto Pick, who in his turn brought attention to the brothers Čapek, František Langer, and Otakar Březina. Other writers belonging to the category of Czechoslovakian mediators between Czech and German culture are Franz Werfel, Egon Erwin Kisch, and Willy Haas, for instance. These writers had supranational loyalty; they were creators of high culture and lived in a hybrid space between Czech and German culture, typically in Prague, which used its own dialect (Prague German) of the German language. At the same time, post-WWI nationalism (in response to the end of Austrian suppression) and antisemitism were growing in the country;

---

[8]   Edward Said, *Representations of the Intellectual* (New York: Pantheon Books, 1994), 49.

and, of course, only a few decades later, Nazism swept through Europe.[9]

The question of identity is also intimately related to that of exile, given the fact that it has a close connection with the oppression of the individual by various social communities, growing bureaucratization, and globalization. As Adorno points out, "for many people it is already an impertinence to say I."[10] The individual is oppressed and displaced. This loss of individuality is brilliantly portrayed in the Czech American exile writer Egon Hostovský's work (see below). Exile becomes an act, a way to assert one's own identity against that of a group or nation.

David Kettler poses an interesting question on the limits of exile.[11] While he contends that the study of diaspora and identity are nowadays more important than ever, he adds that "[t]here are also the perceived homogenizing effects of globalization that seem to be rendering the political concept of exile irrelevant. How can one be in exile in such a world? Perhaps exile is no longer relevant?"[11] Twenty-first-century globalization does indeed appear to diminish the sense of exile, as it is much easier to belong to a less narrowly defined community (the idea of nation, for example, may lose its power), yet globalization brings with itself its own forms of oppression as it strips individuals of their identity. The typical person still thinks of their identity in national or even regional terms—in terms of customs, history, culinary culture, and so forth. These are rendered largely insignificant by globalization.

One can be exiled not only from a place one considers home, but also from a time that seemed meaningful. Such was the case for Johannes Urzidil, for instance, who was forced to emigrate from his native Bohemia which was subsequently permanently changed

---

[9] See, for example, Hillel J. Kieval, "Choosing to Bridge: Revisiting the Phenomenon of Cultural Mediation," *Bohemia Band* 46 (2005): 15–27.

[10] Theodor Adorno, *Minima Moralia: Reflections from Damaged Life* (New York: Verso, 1978), 50.

[11] David Kettler and Zvi Ben-Dor, "Introduction: The Limits of Exile," *Journal of the Interdisciplinary Crossroads* 3, no. 1 (2006): 1–9.

by WWII. Authors like Urzidil tend to create an imaginary home in their dreams and writing.

We shall now look in depth at the themes that twentieth-century Jewish writers, in their attempts to reflect on the condition of exile, address in their work—paying special attention to literary form. We shall focus in the main on authors who used German as their literary language and lived mainly in Eastern and Central Europe due to the fact that German was common among Jewish writers residing in these countries in the first half of the twentieth century. Those using Yiddish, Czech, Polish, Italian, and French will also be included. I analyze prose writers almost exclusively, as poets deserve their own study. Finally, it is important to note that the line of external exile we observe among the writers covered typically moves geographically and historically from the East to the West.

1. Exile as Expulsion and Wandering: Joseph Roth, Sholem Aleichem, Stefan Zweig

The first topic that offers itself in the time frame and geographical location that this study focuses on is the topic of expulsion and wandering, which was so significant in Eastern Europe in the late nineteenth and early twentieth centuries. This subject was first brilliantly examined in Joseph Roth's *The Wandering Jews* (1927). "Wandering" is, so to speak, the most basic, literal, common, and seemingly innocent meaning or manifestation of exile—although in its link with "expulsion" it already intimates something much darker. Expulsion is forced or voluntary, but in both cases it is a drastic human predicament and is undertaken only under extreme duress.

Joseph Roth (b. 1894 in Brody, d. 1939 in Paris), hailing from Ukraine and making it first to Berlin (1925) and later to Paris (1933), became well known for his essays (collected in *The Wandering Jews*), which were written in German. He grew up in Brody, a small town near Lemberg in East Galicia, in the easternmost area of what was then the Austro-Hungarian Empire, now Lviv (Ukraine). The town had a large Jewish population at the time. Roth went to school in Lemberg, which was controlled by the Polish aristocracy despite the fact that the population was mostly Ukrainian (Ruthenian). Roth then moved to Vienna and Berlin, where he worked as an extremely successful liberal journalist for prominent newspapers (*Neue Berliner Zeitung* and *Frankfurter Zeitung*); and after Hitler became chancellor in 1933 he settled in Paris where he continued to be very successful, but became a heavy drinker. He died prematurely in 1939 at the age of forty-four, collapsing after hearing the news that the playwright Ernst Toller, another fellow émigré, had hanged himself in New York. Thus, his life, not only his writing, reflects the East-West wandering of Jews and its often tragic conclusion.

The mass emigration of the Galician peasantry that Roth describes in his work, though, had already occurred in the 1880s — to imperial Germany and later overseas to the United States, Canada, and Brazil. This great *economic* migration lasted until WWI. After the war, Galicia was a victim of hostilities between Ukrainians and Poles, later occupied by Hitler, and then decimated by the Soviet authorities. These events led to mass killings, massacres, and large-scale deportations to Siberia.

When the Austro-Hungarian Empire was dismembered and the map of Eastern Europe redrawn along ethnic lines, the Jews became technically homeless, as there was no territory they could point to as ancestrally their own. The supranational imperial state had suited them, as they could blend in as one of many nations and feel legitimate, at home. The cataclysmic economic crisis of 1929 brought another severe blow. Some began to look to Palestine as a national home, others turned to the supranational creed of communism. Nostalgia for a lost past and anxiety about a homeless future are at the heart of the mature work of Joseph Roth.

In 1932, in the preface to *The Radetzky March* (1932), Roth wrote: "I loved this fatherland. It permitted me to be a patriot and a citizen of the world at the same time, and among all the Austrian peoples also a German. I loved the virtues and merits of this fatherland, and today, when it is dead and gone, I even love its flaws and weaknesses."[12] *The Radetzky March* is an elegy to the cosmopolitan world of Habsburg Austria, as seen by someone from an outlying imperial territory — a great German novel by a writer with barely a toehold in the German community of letters. While Roth indulged his nostalgia for his Austrian fatherland, his wife became mentally ill and was murdered by the Nazis when they invaded Austria.

Roth rejected both fascism and communism; he proclaimed himself a Catholic and involved himself in unsuccessful royalist politics. His ambivalence toward Western civilization led him

---

[12]   Joseph Roth, *The Radetzky March* (London: Granta, 2002).

increasingly to draw on the heritage of Eastern European story-telling. When asked by a friend why he drank so much, he replied, "Do you think you are going to escape? You too are going to be wiped out."

In his essays in *The Wandering Jews*, Roth masterfully depicts the experiences of expelled East European Jews—those who escaped the pogroms and misery in the aftermath of the Russian Revolution and WWI, and who tried to carve out a life for themselves in one of the Central or Western European countries. Expulsion, for Roth, is a harsher version of exile. In his moving book, we learn how countries differed in their reluctant acceptance of these refugees and how difficult it was for the expelled to find anywhere to live. The book is written for Western readers who "feel they might have something to learn from the East and who have perhaps already sensed that great people and great ideas—great but also useful (to them)—have come from Galicia, Russia, Lithuania, and Romania," writes Roth in his introduction.[13]

According to Roth, the Jews have few choices, as they are desperately trying to simply survive:

> The Eastern Jew looks to the West with a longing that it really doesn't merit. To the Eastern Jew, the West signifies freedom, justice, civilization, and the possibility to work and develop his talents. The West exports engineers, automobiles, books, and poems to the East. It sends propaganda soaps and hygiene, useful and elevating things, all of them beguiling and come-hitherish to the East. To the Eastern Jew, Germany, for example, remains the land of Goethe and Schiller, of the German poets, with whom every keen Jewish youth is far more conversant than our own swastika's secondary school pupils.[14]

Roth anatomizes Jewish life in Berlin, Paris, Vienna, and America, and also provides an idealized portrayal of their life in the Soviet Union, where he believes antisemitism has been extinguished by communism. At the same time, he blames Western

---

[13]   Joseph Roth, *The Wandering Jews* (New York: Norton, 2001), 2.

[14]   Ibid., 5–6.

European Jews for losing their Jewishness, tradition, and religion in an effort to assimilate and have a better life. He describes their sense of homelessness, the constant abuse by authorities, the poverty. He contrasts life in the West with that in the shtetl. Whereas the shtetl provided a strong sense of community due to Jews sharing a faith in God and a deeply rooted religious culture, the key elements of which were charity and education, the Jewish ghetto is mainly a part of a city, where Jews are forced to live together as a result of social, legal, and economic pressures. Roth talks about the magic rabbis, the Yiddish theater, and the role of the cantors, all of which are elements of the shtetl that the ghetto has imported; but in the ghetto, Jews have only two possible careers—peddler and installment seller.

WWI brought many Jews to Vienna, as they were entitled to support there because their home countries were occupied; Berlin, on the other hand, was mostly a city of transit for them; Paris was challenging because of the language, but life was better for Jews there, as they blended in better with the population, the city was more international city, and the police relatively benign; Spain was worrisome because of the medieval expulsion; and Poland imposed quotas in universities. Finally, although the quotas were small and more paperwork was required than for anywhere in Europe, North America meant freedom and a safe distance from past and present persecution,

Jews were antimilitaristic, as for centuries they had not been allowed to fight in an army. There was also little motivation for them to fight for a czar, kaiser, or country that gave them no rights. They were not even attached to their names, as those too had been imposed on them. They often also chose camouflaged names to fit in better.

The Jews of Germany at the time looked down upon Eastern Jews and did not want to associate with them. Eastern Jews were completely homeless and forced to move from one country to another. This created fear, suspicion, hatred, and alienation among the non-Jewish German population that the local Jews wanted to separate themselves from. Eastern Jews were forbidden to do many things and were subjected to many kinds of humiliation; and when

Hitler came to power, the settled German and Austrian Jews who had gone through a long and painstaking process of assimilation found themselves linked to the demonized Jews from the East; they found it almost impossible to imagine leaving the country to which they felt they belonged.

Zionism could not present a global solution to the "Jewish Question" and the host Christian nations of Europe were not mature enough to possess the internal freedom, dignity, and compassion for the plight of others to offer truly equal rights to Jews, who suffered for being different even if no longer identifying with the religion because of which they were being cast out. They no longer knew what it was that defined them. Roth was acutely aware throughout the 1930s that Europe's ethical values had been destroyed and that the continent was on the brink of a physical and moral apocalypse. He also knew that the destruction of the Jews would become a key issue in 1930s Europe.

The wandering and expulsion view of exile begins with Sholem Aleichem's (b. 1859, Pereiaslav Khmelnytskyi, d. 1916, New York City) world-renowned book of stories *Tevye the Dairyman* (1894), written in Yiddish. Aleichem became well known for his description of Jewish life in his native Ukraine. After the 1905 wave of pogroms, he moved to New York and later to Geneva. Jerry Bock's musical *Fiddler on the Roof* (1964), based on Aleichem's stories, was the first commercially successful English-language stage production about Jewish life in Eastern Europe. It is, of course, an Americanized perspective, much lighter and more commercial than the Galician Maurice Schwartz's American film *Tevya* from 1939. In effect, Sholem Aleichem brought the Ukrainian Jewish world to the West.

Wandering, which is the consequence of expulsion or persecution is, in a very different way, also present in Stefan Zweig's (b. 1881 in Vienna, d. 1942 in Petropolis, Brazil) much later autobiographical work *The World of Yesterday* (1942)—a book about European cultural life. It is also about the continent's spiritual demise and the movement of its author from Vienna to Britain, to the US, and finally to Brazil, in order to escape the Nazis. In Brazil, Zweig ended his life in a double suicide with his wife, not being able to bear the destruction of Europe, of a world in which personal freedom meant the highest good on earth. Zweig's environment and style of thinking is that of an assimilated and acculturated Central European Jew, who had once belonged to the highest Austrian society and felt secure, at home, and in a sense part of its establishment, unlike the poor Jews from the East European shtetls with nothing but their religious education, particular way of life, and hope for some kind of happiness in an unknown country. Yet, in the end, he too met the same fate of having to leave his home and culture in order to escape the likely possibility of being murdered. In Europe, there was no country that would accept him, and his search for a new home led him across the ocean.

Expulsion and wandering, so familiar to the Jews, became a common experience under the politically oppressive regimes that plagued Central and Eastern Europe almost until the end of the twentieth century. Cultural and political exile from Russia, Poland, Czechoslovakia, and other Eastern Bloc countries occurred in waves throughout the entire century. Expulsion was sometimes physical, and at other times spiritual. Jews abandoned their countries in search of freedom from psychological, cultural, and intellectual oppression long after WWII, becoming wandering Jews in the broadest sense of the phrase, adopting another home, and in many cases never truly being able to settle properly where they finally found themselves.

The wandering of the Jews, so pervasive in Eastern Europe because of expulsion, economic hardship, or from threats of violence, was replaced during the second part of the twentieth century by migration due to Soviet totalitarian domination of these countries. The earlier wandering thus presents a stark image of the violence and destruction, as well as the moral decay, of twentieth-century Europe. Indeed, it is symbolic of the condition of modern man suffering from the oppression of his identity.

I have outlined above three periods and types of exile which took place in twentieth-century Europe. The first was the late nineteenth-century economic and cultural emigration of East European Jews from the Baltic, Russian, Ukrainian, and Polish territories, some of which constituted Eastern Austria, and from the Soviet Union at the end of WWI. Violence, on the whole, was the main motive for their wandering westwards. The second period was Jews fleeing the Nazis in both the East and West to the Americas during WWII. And finally, the third was the escape of Jews from the Soviet Union and its area of dominion and their exile to Western Europe and America. These waves of exile from Eastern Europe can be further divided into the period before WWI and the interwar period for the East European Jews, while for the Czechs—for example, after the 1948 Communist putsch and after the 1968 Soviet occupation. The exodus was virtually continuous. Where once it was antisemitism, it became a more generalized escape of many nationals from political oppression which singled out anyone with a differing opinion. In short, the Nazi regime opened the door for Soviet totalitarianism to dominate a great area of Europe until almost the end of the twentieth century.

2. Exile as Aesthetic Revolt and an Inward Turn: Hugo von Hofmannsthal, Robert Musil, Hermann Broch

Having reviewed the external/physical wandering and exile that took place in the twentieth century, and its representation in literature, let us now look at a very different form of exile—namely, an exclusive phenomenon we can also conceive of as an aesthetic revolt and an inward turn. An early twentieth-century phenomenon, this inward turn characterizes artistic movements such as Symbolism, Decadence, and Dadaism, that is, forms of artistic expression that seek to withdraw from physical reality and that are directed at highbrow audiences. These movements also reject social norms. Now, of course, we wouldn't want to claim that these aesthetic revolts are merely types of exile (their content is much broader); however, they do represent varieties of removal from everyday reality and from engagement with society and its dominant values. They embrace art for art's sake, occasionally employing extreme forms in order to attempt to discover a unique way to protest mainstream ways of thinking and operating.

Decadence, for instance, creates an artificial paradise in response to ugly, dreary industrial society, as well as against boredom, expected destruction, and against so-called progress and innovation. It is an aesthetic of religion, magic, and rituals. Symbolism, Decadence, Dadaism, and so forth, spread throughout Europe in one shape or another from the turn of the twentieth century until about the mid-twenties. Modernism and the avant-garde expanded the possibilities of artistic creation and perception to an extraordinary degree and represented a number of ways of turning inward and away from society. They are not specific to Jewish literature, but in Vienna, which was a major artistic center at the time, they flourished in large part thanks to Jewish interest and support. Very often, these writers were visionaries expressing a premonition of the destructive forces that were soon to take over Europe.

Let us look at just a few examples.

Hugo von Hofmannsthal (b. 1874 in Vienna, d. 1929 in Vienna) is an influential writer and artist whose work contains an intimation of the downfall and destruction of the Austrian Empire. He was Jewish only through his Jewish grandfather, Isaac Hoffman, who moved to Vienna from Bohemia and established himself in the textile business. Whereas Hofmannsthal was brought up Catholic (part of the family's attempt to assimilate), his wife was fully Jewish. Due to the spiritualizing aspect of his work and aesthetics, he was viewed, however, as a "Jewish artist." Both Zionists and anti-Zionists proudly designated him as a fellow Jew; meanwhile, the antisemitic press smeared him. He co-founded the Salzburg Festival, but the paper *Deutsche Volksruf*, for one, described his play *Salzburg's Great World Theatre* (1922) as "very much in the spirit of his race—everything is distorted by filth." Paradoxically, Hofmannsthal was known for antisemitism himself and worried about his own children developing the Jewish trait of "hyper cleverness."[15] Interestingly, he did not become part of the elite circle of Stefan George. He believed that while art is the most important thing in the life of a creative person, it does not have such meaning for those who are unable to create.

His play *The Tower* (1925) is especially relevant to our study. It depicts the extreme abuse of a human being by another and suggests that, devoid of a Christian mission, modern life is without hope. The hero Sigismund imposes inner exile on himself, a chosen path of an individuality that refuses to participate in the ways of the world, claiming individual choice—rather than social conventions—as an ethical right. For the Neo-Romantic Hofmannsthal, this path ends in

---

15 See Paul Reiter, *Bambi's Jewish Roots and Other Essays on German-Jewish Culture* (New York and London: Bloomsbury, 2015), 152.

his protagonist's death. A free individual of superior consciousness cannot fit into a group, cannot obey its rules, and thus cannot continue living. He would have to live as an outcast, which is not an option for him. The play also shows the readiness with which a crowd can elevate an unknown individual to a God-like standing in order to act out its own aggressive and destructive instincts and have them sanctified. As Hermann Broch writes, *"The Tower* also implies Babel—in which it was no longer possible for anyone to come to an understanding with anyone else."[16]

Hofmannsthal's own fate was the inner exile of a poet with great ambition who could not reach a public—a public that had the level of his creativity and the depth of his insight, and thus could appreciate his unusual genius. The context in which he was developing and writing was Austria, which was decomposing due to its loss of ethical values.

This loss can also be seen in an epic form in the work of two other great Austrian writers of the period, Robert Musil (b. 1880 in Klagenfurt, d. 1942 in Geneva), writer of *The Man without Qualities* (1932) and Hermann Broch (b. 1886 in Vienna, d. 1951 in New Haven, Connecticut), writer of *The Sleepwalkers: A Trilogy* (1931–1932), both of whom were forced into exile after the annexation of Austria by Hitler. Musil spent many of his young years in Hranice, Moravia, where he studied, and later in Berlin. He had to escape eventually because of his opinions and his Jewish wife.

Broch's novel *The Sleepwalkers* (1932) covers essentially the same ground as Musil's *Man without Qualities*, namely the degeneration of values, even though they handle the subject very differently. Broch also portrays the entire epoch in *Hofmannsthal and His Time* (1948), which he wrote at the very end of his life in New Haven. Here he shows his contemporary as someone who has stood, in a vacuum, against the epoch which he describes as "a complete collapse of the old value system, which dissolved piece by piece."[17] The collapse of Austria, for these authors, was a poignant prelude to, and had

---

[16] Hermann Broch, *Hugo von Hofmannsthal and His Time* (Chicago: U. of Chicago, 1984), 95.

[17] Ibid., 116.

ramifications for, the twentieth-century West's ethical dissolution and the apocalypse that followed.

Strikingly, none of the writers mentioned in this section have ever found wide audiences and are read only by select and sophisticated readers. Both Broch and Musil ended their own lives abroad—the former in Switzerland, the latter in the US. Their writing ranges from Expressionist to Modernist, but one thing that is constantly present in both is the disappearance of morality and the concomitant disintegration of society. All three of the above writers are now regarded as Austrian cultural giants, but they could not integrate into the mainstream due to the sophistication of their work, their intensity of feeling, and the depth of their thought. They tower over the mediocrity of the cultural life of the era.

3. Exile as Social Renewal:
Theodor Herzl, Max Nordau

Along with the two most general forms of exile already discussed, turning inward and mere wandering, stands a very concrete type of exile — the concept of exile as a social renewal in the form of Zionism, a Jewish program aimed at escaping Europe's hopelessness, lack of values, and antisemitism by creating a free Jewish society in an entirely different geographical area, a homeland where Jews could truly realize themselves without fear, limitations, poverty, killing, and humiliation. This version of the concept of exile is the opposite of the aesthetic one and turning within. It is an outgrowth of the wandering, or its correction or continuance, which is based on a hope that it is possible to end exile permanently. Uri Zilbersheid suggests that Zionism is a multidimensional Jewish revival, and not merely a political matter.[18]

The personalities of certain thinkers stand out, notably those of Theodor Herzl (b. 1860 in Pest, d. 1904 in Reichenau an der Rax), author of *The Jewish State* (1895) and Max Nordau (b. 1849 in Pest, d. 1923 in Paris), author of *The Conventional Lies of Our Civilization* (1883) and *Degeneration* (1892), both born in Budapest and later moving to Vienna and Paris. They were the co-founders of the World Zionist Organization (1897) and co-creators of modern Zionism.

Zionism as an idea, then, has existed since the end of the nineteenth century, yet only certain layers of the Jewish population were originally able to identify with it and save their lives through it. Zionism represented a voluntary, chosen exile, a journey to

---

[18] Uri Zilbersheid, "The Utopia of Theodor Herzl," *Israel Studies* 9, no. 2 (2004): 80.

a faraway country, based on what seemed to some a utopian idea. While it has saved many lives in its time, it has not brought substantial peace for Jews even one hundred twenty years later. It has given birth to new manifestations of antisemitism around the world. Both Herzl and Nordau came to it after unsuccessfully trying to implement the idea of Jewish emancipation and assimilation and witnessing the mass rallies in Paris following the Dreyfus treason trial (1894), during which many chanted "Death to the Jews!" in the streets. This was especially significant, as France was often seen as the model of the modern, enlightened state—after all, it had emancipated the Jews in the aftermath of the revolution. The country established them as equal citizens to Frenchmen. Napoleon overrode old laws restricting Jews to ghettos, lifted laws banning Jews' right to own property and engage in certain professions. Judaism, in fact, became one of the official religions in France. In short, although emancipation and equality were written into the statute books of Europe, antisemitism was still alive in popular social consciousness, with the exception of Britain—likely due to its Protestantism, fundamental liberalism, lower Jewish population, and suspicion of Catholicism.

It was then that Herzl and Nordau conceived of the idea that Jews must leave Europe and found their own state. Herzl was probably even more influenced by the rise to power of the antisemite Karl Lueger in Vienna in 1895. It was then that he stopped believing that antisemitism could ever be eradicated or cured. Europe is, after all, chiefly Christian, and the religion's representatives from its beginnings have accused Jews of deicide.

Herzl made unsuccessful political and diplomatic efforts to secure some land where Jews could settle. He put in writing a detailed and masterful plan for the organization of the future democratic Jewish nation-state. It was to be a progressive, multilingual democracy, where essentially all would be taken care of. It would be a state that would even benefit European Christians, who would move into positions vacated by emigrating Jews and secure formerly Jewish property at very advantageous prices. The welfare state and the subsequent stateless society that Herzl proposed testify, according to Zilbersheid, "to his deep connection with the utopian tradition."[19] Herzel's vision drew on Western cosmopolitanism rather than the Eastern European nation-oriented Zionism proposed by Ahad Ha'am, who "saw no point in any political solution that was divorced from a national solution."[20]

Herzl's daughter died in the concentration camp Theresienstadt with her husband in 1943. Upon learning of his parents' fate, his grandchild, who was sent to England in 1935, where he became a captain in the British army, committed suicide by jumping from the Massachusetts Avenue Bridge in Washington, DC in 1946.

Nordau was central to the eleven World Zionist Congresses, which played a vital part in shaping what Zionism would become. As a critic of the West, he acutely characterized the European *fin-de-siècle* as an illness caused by degeneration and hysteria. In this respect, Nordau was an anti-aesthetic thinker who did not understand and appreciate the artistic innovations of his time. He was, though, a great supporter of Theodor Herzl's approach to Zionism.

His book *Die konventionellen Lügen der Kulturmenschheit* (1883) attacks all aspects of civilization—religion, monarchy, aristocracy, politics, economics, marriage, and so on, as lies that trap people and make them live inauthentic and embittered lives. Austrian official decree may have condemned the book, but *Die konventionellen Lügen der Kulturmenschheit* prophesied the disaster to come. Nordau believed in emigration as a solution to survival itself, as well as a solution to the economic problems associated with industrial society. In his attitudes toward art and women he is, however, extremely narrow-minded and moralistic.

Both Herzl and Nordau were attacked for ignoring Jewish spiritual values. Their idea was to build a tolerant secular society in Israel, escape the industrialization of Europe, and return to their historically native soil. Eastern Jews, more in touch with Jewish spiritual values, opposed this. Spirituality—occultism, magic,

---

[19]   Ibid.: 81.

[20]   Yossi Goldstein, "Eastern Jews vs. Western Jews: The Ahad Ha'am-Herzl Dispute and Its Cultural and Social Implications," *Jewish History* 24, nos. 3/4 (2010): 364.

theosophy, and so forth— was common at this time in Europe; however, a lack of faith prevailed. Zionism in the work of Herzl and Nordau represented a new kind of Jewish wandering, with a distinct humanitarian program and rejection of the religious definition of Jewishness. Its influence was vast and longstanding. The trauma of the Holocaust propelled many Jewish thinkers to insist on the creation of a land in which Jews would be legally protected. The purpose of Zionism was to end wandering and find a permanent home, where Jews would no longer be ostracized. Many have actually found true purpose in reaching this goal, even if its broad, permanent, peaceful, and unifying resolution has still remained only a hope. In effect, regardless of the founding of the State of Israel, wandering has remained the more permanent state of affairs for Jews.

4. Exile as Resistance and a Moral Stance: Karl Kraus, Arthur Schnitzler

Let us now return to the more intrinsic components of exile, such as those represented in the work of two Austrian literary giants of the early twentieth century, Karl Kraus and Arthur Schnitzler. Like Hofmannsthal, Musil, and Broch, they were profoundly critical of the society in which they lived. However, their criticism is not of a philosophical and abstract character; rather, it consists of a direct criticism of society and a realistic depiction of its troubling condition. Furthermore, instead of being largely ignored, their ideas were regarded as scandalous.

The ingenious Karl Kraus (b. 1874 in Jičín, d. 1936 in Vienna), hailing from Bohemia but settling in the cultural mecca of the time, Vienna, published his famous experimental and extensive play *The Last Days of Mankind* in 1919. Standing against a decaying European civilization with his sharp and relentless wit, Kraus expressed the form of exile as a resistance to the value system, or a lack thereof, of European society. A similar type of exile, a distinctively moral stance, is presented in Arthur Schnitzler's (b. 1862 in Vienna, d. 1931 in Vienna) novel *Professor Bernhardi* (1912). Both *The Last Days of Mankind* and *Professor Bernhardi*, like the authors discussed in the previous chapters, explore the alienation of values. The struggle against the society's immorality is clearly a lost cause for the heroes of all these works; however, they insist on sustaining a certain moral stance, which excludes them from society and makes outcasts of them.

Karl Kraus was an uncompromising critic of practically everything Austrian, from politics to psychoanalysis, to Zionism, nationalism, economic policies, and corruption: "Kraus wrote as if Zionism was merely another fad, invented by 'Ringstrasse' dandies like Herzl, to whom he objected first and foremost as a 'littérateur' of the 'Young Vienna' school and as a journalist of the 'Neue Freie Presse.'"[21] He was for decades an intimate friend of the famed Czech aristocrat Sidonie Nádherná, who never married him, possibly succumbing to the opinion of her other important literary friend, Rainer Maria Rilke, who was objecting to Kraus's "unrepeatable difference" (considered to be a euphemism for Jewishness). Kraus was a member of the bohemian circle Jung Wien (with Herzl, Hofmannsthal, Zweig, and Schnitzler), which met at Café Griensteidl, later in Café Central. In 1899, he founded his own newspaper *Die Fackel* (The Torch). From 1911, the newspaper was written by him exclusively until his death in 1936.

He was also an influential speaker. At the peak of his popularity, his lectures attracted up to 4,000 people and *Die Fackel* sold 40,000 copies. We cannot, then, put him exactly into the category of outsider. His masterpiece *The Last Days of Mankind* (1919) is a large satirical play about WWI. The play combines dialogue from contemporary documents with apocalyptic fantasy and commentary by two characters called "the Grumbler" and "the Optimist." The play was self-published in *Die Fackel* and its first performance was in Turin in 1991, long after Kraus's death. Yet, although it only appeared in his newspaper, it stimulated a new type of documentary theater in 1920s Germany. The play was an ethical protest and Kraus refused to let it be turned into a spectacle. His emphasis was on poetry, not on theatrical effects and entertainment.

Kraus also wrote a satire on the Nazis, *The Third Walpurgis Night* (1933), which he was afraid to publish, only printing extracts from it in *Die Fackel* under the title *Why the Torch Does Not Appear* in 1936. He abandoned Judaism in 1911 and became a Catholic; but in 1923, due to the Church's support for Hitler, he abandoned Catholicism as well. He was a meticulous user of language, as well as a critic

---

21   Robert S. Wistrich, "Karl Kraus: Jewish Prophet or Renegade?," *European Judaism: A Journal for the New Europe* 9, no.2 (Summer 1975): 33.

of it. Language was extremely important to him. He wrote: "Language is the mother of thought, not its handmaiden."

Kraus's criticism of humanity is thorough and relentless. He is even such a critic of Jews that many consider him to be a Jewish antisemite. His form is avant-garde and replete with estrangements, such as making documents into characters and emphasizing that words have the same level of culpability as deeds. He portrays the terrible moral decay of his society, which spreads hatred regardless of the toll it will take; he stands at the very center of a society, yet in total opposition to it; he shows how the perversity of propaganda leads to brutality and sadism. Ignorance is rampant, he argues. His expressionistic drama is constructed from documents and events, while apparitions raise it to a transcendent place where God passes judgment on mankind as deserving of total annihilation for its desecration of nature, human, and animal life, as well as its utter inhumanity.

Kraus acts as the moral conscience of humanity, unveiling its ignorant illusions and their horrifying consequences. His work is prophetic and gives the moral stance rendered in Hofmannsthal's *Tower* a global dimension. Having been an extremely popular satirist, Kraus represents the extreme end of the concept of exile since he condemns humanity to extinction. His play is extremely successful as theatre because of its multiple juxtapositions, contrasts, and rich visual effects. The perversity of humanity, however, leading to apocalyptic despair is *The Last Days of Mankind*'s central theme. Kraus's method is very complex, shifting from expressionism to surrealism (e.g. the transformation of humans into animals). The play is a montage of heterogeneous materials and was eventually staged at the end of the twentieth century all over the world. It is now recognized as a masterpiece.

Arthur Schnitzler was a realistic writer, a master of micro-fiction and humor, and the first to write German stream-of-consciousness narration. Kraus and Schnitzler were essentially enemies. Schnitzler provoked Vienna society first with his frank, amoral descriptions of sexuality, which evoked admiration even from Freud (e.g. *Reigen* [1897]). His work was so scandalous that it was more famous for being banned than for being staged. His stories are mostly elegies for a vanished world that often end in suicide. His daughter actually committed suicide Schnitzler died of a brain hemorrhage three years after her death.

Later in life, Schnitzler also took a strong stand against antisemitism in the play *Professor Bernhardi* (1912), where he dissects Austrian antisemitism and its insidious, multiple forms. While Herzl views antisemitism as a political and social issue, Schnitzler sees it as a psychological question and a private experience. In his work, Schnitzler takes the position of a west Austrian Jew, who considers himself as more Austrian than Jewish, yet he always feels a deep sense of isolation and confusion regarding his identity. For such a Jew, Herzl's solution of abandoning his home country and starting a new life in a faraway nationally defined country is not practical.

In *Professor Bernhardi*, the various characters express respect for the Jewish protagonist Bernhardi, the chair of a private medical institute in Vienna, but they actually orchestrate his downfall because of their maddening half-heartedness. Such half-heartedness in moral attitudes was characteristic of Vienna at the turn of the century. Bernhardi, who loses his position due to his ethical stance protecting a patient's well-being against a Catholic priest, becomes completely disillusioned with human society, its indifference, which only too readily concedes its own weakness and adopts an attitude of resigned self-irony. This corrupt world contaminates pure individuals. Rather than engaging in politics, Bernhardi chooses to go to prison, which he finds completely embarrassing. He takes a public stand, but refuses to bastardize it by having it misused by press and political parties for their own purposes. The social process makes nonsense out of Bernhardi's attempt at consistency and integrity. Passionate moral despair thus results. At the same time, the greatness of Schnitzler's art consists in him not intruding with an explicit critical voice in the play. As Schlein notes, "it is this very lack of intrusion and explicit criticism that make his works doubly effective."[22] The play also portrays the impossibility of forming a commitment to wider society for Jews, due to their

---

[22]   Rena A. Schlein, "The Motif of Hypocrisy in the Works of Arthur Schnitzler," *Modern Austrian Literature* 2, no. 1 (Spring 1969): 28.

general nonacceptance as well as an acute sense of isolation of a morally oriented individual.

Schnitzler's works were called "Jewish filth" by Adolf Hitler and were banned by the Nazis in Austria and Germany. In 1933, when Joseph Goebbels organized book burnings in Berlin and other cities, Schnitzler's works were thrown into the flames along with those of other Jews, such as Einstein, Marx, Kafka, Freud, and Stefan Zweig.

5. Exile as Gender Marginalization and the Independence of the Femme Fatale: Alma Mahler

While Karl Kraus had the strength to laugh out loud at his society and was a very popular writer during his lifetime, suicide became a mass phenomenon in Austria. As we have seen, many male writers were open critics and analysts of society and even if scandalized or marginalized, they often had the opportunity to contribute and make a name for themselves. Women in general were, on the other hand, completely marginalized in early twentieth-century European culture and were frequently cast in the role of the *femme fatale*, which represented a male fantasy, giving women an illusion of power in a *de facto* completely male-dominated world. This is shown in Zweig's *The World of Yesterday*, and was the fate of Alma Mahler (b. 1879 in Vienna, d. 1964 in New York City), who became famous as the wife of the late Romantic Austro-Bohemian Jewish composer Gustav Mahler, later the German Bauhaus architect Walter Gropius, and finally the Prague-born Austrian Jewish writer Franz Werfel. While she was a composer in her own right, only seventeen of her songs survive, and she is mainly remembered as the wife of three prominent men of the period (as well as the lover of Klimt, Kokoshka, and Zemlinsky). If she hadn't associated with these prominent men, she would have been completely unknown to the world. On the other hand, we would be hard-pressed to find a man who is well known solely for associating with famous women artists.

Gender marginalization is thus another invisible form of exile, greatly affecting women as late as the twentieth century, even though progress was slowly being made in their social inclusion. Let us not forget that gender marginalization concerns a full half of the population at any given time. The fact that we cannot cite an author as important in this period as the men discussed above speaks for itself. Indeed, when Alma married Mahler, it was under the condition that she would forgo her interest in composing. According to Françoise Giroud, by the age of twenty Alma had written more than a hundred songs, some instrumental pieces, and the outline of an opera, but she spent her life making copies of her husband's scores. At the same time, she never acknowledged Mahler's artistic greatness and felt sporadically antisemitic and superior to him due to her Christianity.[23] She also failed to understand Gropius's genius. She seriously hesitated about whether to marry the third genius, Franz Werfel, who irritated her with his Jewishness, according to Françoise Giroud.

She even transferred this antisemitism to her own children, openly appreciating her daughter by Gropius above her daughter by Mahler due to her Aryan features.[24] Alma also fell in love with a priest who was an admirer of Hitler and both she and Werfel initially considered Hitler to be a genuine German idealist— a position unthinkable for Jews during the 1930s.[25] Both Gropius and Alma independently ended up in the US, where the former had another successful career, while Alma considered her exile a disease. She eventually took to alcohol and died in New York in 1964.

Women were considered to be free in Viennese society, while at the same time a destructive and distracting influence on talented men. Otto Weininger's *Sex and Character*, for example, contrasts heroic virility with abject femininity.[26] Jews are grouped in the

---

[23] See Françoise Giroud, *Alma Mahler or the Art of Being Loved* (Oxford: Oxford UP, 1991), 50.

[24] Ibid., 138.

[25] Ibid., 139.

[26] See Otto Weininger, *Sex and Character* (London and New York: G. P. Putnam's Sons, 1906), 117-123, 146, 186-188. Throughout his book, Weininger asserts that women and Jews are inferior beings, which need to be transformed. The Jews must rise above Judaism and become Christians and women must be morally saved by men.

same bag with women: dishonest, materialistic, prone to trickery. It was only in 1897 that a woman was admitted to the Faculty of Medicine at the University of Vienna. The image of the *femme fatale* as an enchantress, vampire, monster, or demon, using coercion and lies to achieve her purpose, resonates with the Jewish stereotype. Jewishness was often identified with femininity and *vice versa*. The *femme fatale*, according to Barbara Hales, during this period was often demonized as a criminal, masculine, and diseased.[27] She also points out that the image of the femme fatale is a "marker of loss and exile's inner turmoil," as seen especially in film noir.[28]

This fundamental marginalization of women is akin to the marginalization of Jews as a whole in the early twentieth century and in particular those writers who freely expressed their opinions about the decay of Viennese society. Jews were feared and looked down upon as feminine, among other things, due to their predominant interest in matters intellectual and spiritual, while women were feared for their femininity and sexuality. The *femme fatale* was also a threat to the traditional idea of women because of her independence. It is, then, easy to see the common denominator among these seemingly very different types of people and issues, namely, the concept of exile as independence—a threat to the self-image of the nation, not to speak of a threat to the male ego.

In modern times, women's social standing continues to be invisible in the context of studies of exile, as the concept is typically tied to that of the nation. Eva C. Karpinski writes:

> When exile's association with nationalism is made to be "essential," as in Said, women's experiences usually tend to be erased. However, one can say as well that exile, linked to passivity and waiting, has already been feminized in patriarchal discourses which have often practiced exclusion through feminization.[29]

---

[27] Barbara Hales, "Projecting Trauma: The Femme Fatale in Weimar and Hollywood Film Noir," *Women in German Yearbook* 23 (2007): 224–243.

[28] Ibid., 239.

[29] Eva C. Karpinski, "Choosing Feminism, Choosing Exile: Towards the Development of a Transnational Feminist Consciousness," in *Émigré*

On the other hand, Karpinski notes that recently "[t]here has been a notable change of attitude in feminist critics' thinking about exile. From reading women's exile as a stigma of marginality, they have moved on to embracing exile as a 'privileged' location from which to question the dominant order."[30]

Thus, writers and women in exile no longer appear today as weak, people to be ignored and pitied, but individuals with a strong identity and, due to their outsider status, the ability to critically observe and evaluate society.

Feminism. Transnational Perspectives, ed. Alena Heitlinger (Toronto: U. of Toronto Press, 1999), 24.

[30]   Ibid., 24.

6. Exile as an Escape from Patriarchal Oppression: Franz Werfel

Another topic which plays an important role in Central European literature of the early twentieth century is the topic of escape from patriarchal oppression. This form of exile is almost as common as the marginalization of women. Patriarchal oppression appears often in literary works of the period. One of the best examples is Franz Werfel's novella *Not the Murderer* from 1919. It shows the perversity of the structure of the family (largely German) of the time. In the novel, the father is an extremely oppressive figure who thwarts the life of his son, as well as the rest of the family. By pointing to this behavior, Franz Werfel reveals himself to be an early feminist.

Franz Werfel (b. 1890 in Prague, d. 1945 in Beverly Hills) became known in America as the author of the *Song of Bernadette* (1941); however, he was a versatile poet, novelist, playwright, as well as the author of historical novels such as *The Forty Days of Musa Dagh* (1930) — a story about the Armenian Genocide, an account of an extraordinary military operation, of a successful resistance to tyranny, and a tribute to religious fervor. Werfel was also the writer of fine biographical novels like *Verdi* (1924) and *Jeremiah* (1937), and political and humorous plays like *Jacobowski and the Colonel* (1944), which dealt with the topic of escape into exile. He encountered Armenian refugees in the 1930s during his journey to the Middle East and became a refugee from Hitler soon after, ending his life in Los Angeles with Alma Mahler-Werfel by his side. His late works were turned into films in the US, yet he spent his last years in California in the throes of depression.

Werfel originally belonged to the circle of Kafka, Buber, and Brod in Prague and was an outspoken pacifist. He served in the Austrian army on the Russian front and was eventually condemned for treason for his outspoken pacifism. His poems about the war appeared in 1919 under the title *Der Gerichtstag* (The Day of Judgment) and revealed his despair for humanity. Although he renounced his Jewishness in 1929 in order to marry Mahler, he still had to leave Vienna after the Anschluss in 1938 in fear for his life. He left for France but had to flee from there after the German occupation. With the assistance of the Emergency Rescue Committee in Marseille, he and Alma narrowly escaped the Nazis and traveled to the United States.

While in France, Werfel made a visit to the shrine of the Our Lady of Lourdes, where he found spiritual solace. He also received help from the Catholic order that staffed the shrine. This led him to writing *The Song of Bernadette*, which made him famous in the US. He also wrote poetry, plays, and novels that dealt with music, history, and the Catholic faith. He supposedly, however, only converted to Catholicism just before his death in 1945. In spite of his belief in the ultimate triumph of the spiritual, his later works are pessimistic, with the exception of the lighthearted *Jacobowski and the Colonel*. Werfel had previously rejected political and social change as futile due to the flawed nature of humanity. According to his philosophy, only an individual's spiritual values could ultimately triumph. His solution was to magnify divine mystery and the holiness of mankind.

This approach was especially appreciated in his new homeland, America. *The Song of Bernadette* was eventually made into a successful Hollywood film in 1943 and won three Oscars. While both Werfel and Kraus became renegades from the Jewish faith and turned, at least temporarily, to Catholicism, there was nevertheless a big difference between their worldviews. Edward Timms writes, "Dismayed by the conduct of the Churches during the war, Kraus had no confidence in the ideal of Christian love, so blithely espoused by Werfel as he gravitated towards Catholicism. Thus Kraus defended the rule of law as a Jewish heritage with political significance.[31]

---

[31]   Edward Timms, *Karl Kraus, Apocalyptic Satirist: The Post-War Crisis and the Rise of the Swastika* (New Haven: Yale UP, 2005), 245.

Werfel's early novella *Not the Murderer* (1937) portrays the society he has been born into that was the root of much more malignant forms of exile to appear imminently. *Not the Murderer* is about a boy Karl who grows up with a cold, authoritarian father, who constantly puts him down in order to build his own self-esteem, which rests on military honors and rigid discipline. The father makes it all the way to general, but his wife and child live loveless lives. The wife becomes an obsessive cleaner and eventually dies. The boy becomes a cadet, then an officer in the army, but grows more and more insecure and bitter. He has no life, no woman, no confidence, no joy. He lives only through duty and fear of his father. He is subjected to constant humiliations and lives in squalor.

Karl's life improves only when a deaf-mute man he socializes with introduces him to a group of Russian anarchists. This group first involves him in spying on the military and then in a plot to assassinate the Russian tsar. His father's abusive behavior increases. Eventually, after an especially cruel episode, Karl decides to murder his father—but he fails, as he takes pity on his father. As a result, he receives only nine months of incarceration. After that, Karl moves to Hamburg and eventually to America, where he gets married. There, he develops the theory that every evil in society is due to patriarchy, of fathers oppressing sons because they do not feel love for their families. Fathers force their sons into a hateful structure of activity simply to serve themselves. If mothers were in charge, the author believes, they would act out of knowledge and love, as they are emotionally closer to their children. As it is, the whole social system is based on rotten male domination. In *Not the Murderer*, Werfel presents himself as a revolutionary social reformer, as well as an early feminist, a relatively unnoticed side of him due to his more famous prose works. America appears in his novella as a dreamworld, where things are going to be good. It is a place of escape from oppression and depicted optimistically, if vaguely.

7. Exile as Anxiety and Involuntary Memory: Franz Kafka, Sigmund Freud, Marcel Proust, Bruno Schulz

We find another form of exile when we study the work of (for many) the number one Czech Jewish German author of the twentieth century, Franz Kafka (b. 1883 in Prague, d. 1924 in Kierling, Austria). His work has been written about from many different points of view and, therefore, I will limit myself here to the subject of inner exile, namely Kafka's well-known propensity for anxiety. How else should we read him? Kafka generally shows that "man's life is only a shadow and true reality lies elsewhere, in the inaccessible, in the inhuman or the suprahuman"[32]—a life that is dehumanized by the dead hand of bureaucracy. Anxiety clearly is a significant feature of exile, whether one is excluded, or excludes oneself from wider society by claiming one's difference and independence. It causes anxiety for the exile, first of all, by their being, so to speak, cast out of life: this is naturally anxiety-producing and Kafka was one of the first to describe this condition plaguing modern man. For Milan Kundera, Kafka's work is an example of "radical autonomy."[33]

The texture of anxiety is especially well portrayed in Kafka's novel *Amerika* (1927). The novel is the tale of a European émigré, Karl Rossmann, and permeated with a feeling of anxiety—the core of all Kafka's work. *Amerika* is a bildungsroman, a picaresque story, a dark vision of modern civilization that is filled with alienation and cruelty. His hero is a young man who is sent to America by his parents as punishment for impregnating a maid. Prague was to

[32] Milan Kundera, "Kafka's World," *The Wilson Quarterly* 12, no. 5 (Winter 1988): 99.

[33] Ibid.: 91.

Kafka a "little mother with claws" and thus not a real homeland. He always dreamed of leaving. Interestingly, in this "novel of leaving" the protagonist carries within himself all the inner anguish Kafka felt in Prague and transfers it to the other country.

The novel was first published in English translation in England in 1938 (translated by Edwin and Willa Muir). It was long dismissed, as it is not based on actual experience of the writer, who never set a foot in America. It is an imaginary story filled with absurd situations, the minute introspection of the narrator, and exaggerated concerns with fairness in the treatment of the powerless. Torturous self-doubt is Karl's constant companion. He is forever speculating why others might be behaving the way they do. He is in a precarious situation as soon as he arrives in America due to his domineering and controlling rich uncle Jakob, with whom he lives at first in New York. Karl merely argues with his uncle once and he is thrown out. Exile, thus, is once again interconnected with the meaning of escaping patriarchal dominance, which we have portrayed in the previous chapter.

Karl connects with two crooks who gradually rob him of all his possessions. When he finally extricates himself from this relationship and finds a modest job at a hotel with the help of an older woman, the crooks quickly compromise him and get him fired. He suffers a verbal beating from the head porter and head waiter, gets chased by the police, and ends up in a submissive relationship with another woman, who is a dictator and makes him into her servant. He finds it very difficult to leave this situation, but he finally succeeds and ends up joining the Theater of Oklahama, which "welcomes anyone." Karl doesn't care what he does; he just wants to settle down somewhere and not be abused. The troupe, though, boards a train and goes on another journey. Life thus appears to be an endless and aimless wandering.

The novel first appeared as a short story "The Stoker" (1913 — the first chapter of the book proper); it also appeared under the title "The Man who Disappeared" (translated into English in 1996 by Michael Hoffmann). The title *Amerika* was chosen by Max Brod after Kafka's death. The novel is both more humorous and more realistic than most of Kafka's other works, and lacks the poetic strength of his well-known dreamlike novels, which do not display the constructive effort of depicting a particular space. It does share a major motif found in Kafka, however: an oppressive and intangible system that repeatedly puts people in bizarre situations. Specifically, within *Amerika*, a scorned individual often has to plead his innocence in front of remote and mysterious figures of authority.

The novel was adapted for the screen as the film *Klassenverhältnisse* (Class Relations) by Jean-Marie Straub and Danièle Huillet in 1984. Federico Fellini's *Intervista* revolves around the fictional filming of the novel's adaptation. In 1994, the Czech director Vladimír Michálek made it into a film and the German artist Martin Kippenberger created a vast installation on the theme at MoMA in 2009 titled *The Happy End of Franz Kafka's "Amerika."* There, America is presented as an immense employment-recruiting center, the biggest mechanized theater in the world, and shows the artist in the modern world as an awkward fighter.

Kafka has been interpreted as a Modernist, Magic Realist, Expressionist, and especially as an Existentialist, due to the apparent hopelessness and absurdity that seems to permeate his writing. Some have tried to locate a Marxist influence in his satire of bureaucracy in stories such as "In the Penal Colony," *The Trial*, and *The Castle*, whereas others have suggested that anarchism is an inspiration for his anti-authority viewpoint. Borges read his work through the lens of Judaism, while others have seen Freudian themes or allegories of a metaphysical quest for God (Thomas Mann, for example) in it. Milan Kundera believes Kafka is a Surrealist humorist. For Gabriel García Márquez, he gives the modern writer a new way to write. His work clearly has a multivalent nature. His descriptions of legal proceedings are actually accurate and reflect the adversarial system of justice customary in German and Austrian courts. We might also keep in mind that all Kafka's major novels were left unfinished and that their definitive versions were created by Max Brod.

Anxiety is not just a characteristic feeling for Kafka's exiled hero: it is the condition of the twentieth-century individual. The great early twentieth-century Viennese psychologist and father of psychoanalysis, Sigmund Freud (b. 1856 in Příbor, Moravia, then Austria, now the Czech Republic, d. 1939 in Hampstead, UK), is interestingly preoccupied with the same feeling, looking for a cure for it in his *The Future of an Illusion* (1927) and *Civilization and Its Discontents* (1930), for example, in which he depicts modern civilization in an unflattering way, namely as something built on people's repressed instincts and religion as an institution based on fear.

Fear of the father is also a major theme in Freud. The image of the protective, but fear-inspiring father is manufactured into the image of God. Nothing in religion is provable and therefore religion raises suspicions. The truth of religious doctrines is based on inner experience, which, however, the majority lacks. Religions are, nevertheless, powerful, as our wish for protection, love, and safety is powerful. Religion is, according to Freud, founded on an illusion and thus on intellectual dishonesty. It creates a prohibition on thought. Yet this "lie" is the only thing that holds our civilization together. Its loss is cruel and means that people no longer feel that there is something solid beneath their feet and have a stabilizing fear of punishment. This state is not, unfortunately, replaced by reason, but by other similar doctrines, characterized by the same attributes: sanctity, rigidity, intolerance, and the prohibition of thought for the system's own defense (see Marxism). Religion is thus a universal obsessional neurosis, which brings people consolation according to Freud. Civilization is based on a thin layer of ideas, which cannot guard us from merciless nature. The fundamental helplessness of man leads to an all-permeating anxiety. Religion, according to Freud, will eventually be discarded and replaced by science, as science is not an illusion, but the gradual discovery of truth.

While Kafka physically wandered just between Prague, Germany, and Austria, Freud, left his life in Vienna and emigrated to London as an eighty-three-year-old man on the brink of WWII. He had struggled to be accepted in Viennese academic society for a long time; however, later in life his theories caused a sensation. Developing psychoanalysis, he published on religion, literature, sexual mores, biography, sculpture, prehistory, and so forth.

Another important Jewish writer, who could be seen as akin to Kafka due to his clear opposition to mainstream social values, and whose work contains a sense of deep anxiety is Marcel Proust

(b. 1871 in Neuilly-Auteuil-Passy, d. 1922 in Paris). His position within the French cultural scene was firmer and more secure than that of Kafka, who was not accepted by Czechs because he spoke and wrote in German, by Germans for being a Jew and living in a Czech-speaking country, and by Jews for not being religious. Nevertheless, we can find certain similarities between these two unusual writers. It is also interesting to look at Proust as the Western counterpart of the Jewish writer/intellectual. He was much less threatened by antisemitism and uprootedness during his lifetime. In fact, he spent a substantial part of his life among the French aristocracy.

Proust was brought up in his father's Catholic faith, even though he ended up as an atheist. His anxiety was not politically or racially motivated, but was of a personal and general human kind (an underlying exclusion from society due to his homosexuality). His response to it involved intense preoccupation with a certain kind of memory (known as involuntary memory) and sense of meaninglessness and disconnectedness from reality. This is reflected especially in his well-known novel in seven volumes *In Search of Lost Time* (1913–1927). He created an intensely private inner world, filled with melancholy and indistinct longing.

A similarly private and intense world is found in the work of the Polish Jewish writer Bruno Schulz (b. 1892 in Drohobych, Ukraine, d. 1942 in Drohobych, Ukraine), another outcast cultivating dreamlike writing. His contemporary, the Prague Jew Johannes Urzidil (b. 1896 in Prague, d. 1970 in Rome), left for America depicting the loss of the world he once thought of as home. Urzidil created a new personal world from memory, fact, and fantasy, a world more true and real, yet saturated with anxiety.

Thus, each of the authors in this section, despite their different social worlds, were preoccupied by a form of anxiety that underlies modern civilization due to extreme isolation.

8. Exile as Doom and Revenge: Hermann Ungar

There is a fine line between anxiety and doom. When anxiety becomes unmanageable, a feeling of doom arises. However, aesthetically a stance can be created from doom—"noble infirmity." This happens in the work of another Moravian by birth, who is much less known than the authors already discussed, Hermann Ungar (b. 1893 in Boskovice, d. 1929 in Prague). Ungar is a dark author whose work takes the sense of exile as far as doom, or noble infirmity, in a way somewhat similar to Marcel Proust. Ungar, unlike Proust, though, is fascinated by extremely abusive behavior and the revenge that can result from such treatment. Interestingly, Ungar's work was immediately noted in France, yet rather neglected in Germany and Czechoslovakia.

Ungar grew up speaking German and Czech and was educated in German, as most Jews in the Czech lands were. He played a significant role in Czech Zionism and confronted the Catholic antisemitic and superstitious bigotry common in the Moravian countryside. During his adolescence, the Hilsner trial[34] was still fresh in peoples' minds and precipitated attacks on Jewish shops and homes in his area. During WWI, he fought on the Russian front and was wounded; after the war, he lost his interest in Zionism and devoted himself to supporting the newly formed Czechoslovakia and its democratic ideals. He died prematurely in 1929 at the age of thirty-six of appendicitis. His family was later deported to Nazi concentration camps, where they perished, except for his sister who

---

[34]　Leopold Hilsner was falsely accused of murdering a Czech girl for ritualistic reasons (1899/1900); he was defended by Thomas Garrigue Masaryk, the future first president of Czechoslovakia.

left for Palestine and committed suicide in 1946 after hearing of her family's fate.

Ungar's literary work was published in editions that were soon forgotten and he was unacknowledged for decades. While Thomas Mann and other major writers and publishers valued his work very highly, Max Brod, who canonized the Prague Circle, on the other hand, mentions Ungar only in passing. In his native land he was published only in 2002–2006 by the American Twisted Spoon Press. Diane George writes:

> He should be considered not only in the context of other Czech German writers (Rilke, Werfel, Paul Leppin) and not only as a lesser or lesser-known Kafka, but also alongside the Austrian Leopold von Sacher Masoch. Many of Ungar's motifs could justly be called masochistic—strippings, beatings, humiliations—but a more important point of comparison is Ungar's and Masoch's use of suspense.[35]

Ungar's *Boys and Murderers* (1920) and *The Maimed* (1922) are stories of oppressed and abused boys who turn into depraved men. In *Boys and Murderers*, the author uses this situation to dissect murderous behavior, dark parts of the human psyche, depravities of the heart, and delusions of the mind. Each story presents a twisted and sadistic individual revenging himself for his lack of love in his early life and his resulting sense of powerlessness and loneliness. Ungar's protagonists project their accumulated hatred onto innocent individuals. Deviant sexual behavior, a disgust for female sexuality, the torture of animals, and the abuse of women are all part of their behavior. In the story "A Man and a Maid," a young man continues his depraved, lonely, heartless, and cruel life in America despite his becoming a successful businessman. In "Story of a Murder," Ungar shows how the contempt and abuse of his father, as well as society, leads a boy to become a murderer. Ungar also brings up the irresistible urge to torture and kill that such men have towards the weak (including animals) or handicapped.

---

[35] Diana George, review of *Boys & Murderers: Collected Short Fiction*, by Hermann Ungar, *Chicago Review* 53, nos. 2/3 (Autumn 2007): 206.

In the novel *The Maimed*, the main hero, Franz Polzer, is just a very frightened individual, who subconsciously replays situations from his childhood, a time when he was deprived of power, dignity, and love. This causes a lack of trust in people and irrational fear of them. His sexuality, a source of shame, leads him to a desperate search for security, which he manifests by endlessly counting his meager possessions. The inability to feel any true feelings and act on them is a gruesome premonition of the horrific civilizational disease that gripped Europe and especially German society in the twentieth century. It is reminiscent of Kafka's absurdist story "In the Penal Colony." Even though America might present a certain freedom or productive way of life to one of Ungar's antiheroes, it really does not free him from his inner hell, as he continues to pursue his destructive lifestyle even there. Compassion is nonexistent in Ungar's protagonists. Thus, when compared with Werfel's antipatriarchal story, we see that Ungar depicts essentially the same issue, but carries it much further in terms of its ominous implications and consequences.

Ungar's and Kafka's protagonists achieve only very limited inner freedom by removing themselves from the causes of their discomfort. While Kafka's writing is abstract and profoundly polysemic, Ungar's writing describes credible, if exaggerated, oppressive human situations. Perhaps a reason for Kafka's enormous world renown is the fact that his stories, despite their darkness, have a humorous streak and can be applied to a broad spectrum of situations, while Ungar's work is rooted in a highly specific environment with protagonists that are naturalistically depicted and denies the possibility of redemption. Ungar's protagonists are marginal and their behavior distasteful, yet this very same behavior became mainstream only a few years later as the Nazis dominated Europe.

9. Exile as a Loss of Identity: Saul Friedländer

An entirely new chapter in the character of exile starts with WWII, as reality became almost unrecognizable for Europeans, and for Jews especially. We can speak here of a loss of identity on a global scale through utter abandonment, anguish, defenselessness, and dehumanization, which take many important forms that, however, have one thing in common—a loss of faith leading to the hardening of the human heart.

The issue of the loss of identity is brilliantly exemplified in the work of the historian Saul Friedländer (born 1932 in Prague). Friedländer grew up in France and survived the occupation as a child in a Catholic boarding school near Vichy (1942–1944), while his parents were arrested by Vichy French gendarmes, turned over to the Germans, and gassed at Auschwitz. He got to know about the death of his parents and about his Jewish provenience only in 1946. He became a Zionist and emigrated to Israel in 1948. He then studied political science in Paris in the fifties and became an assistant to Shimon Peres, then vice-minister of defense of Israel. He received a Ph.D. in Geneva in 1963 and taught there until 1988, when he became a professor of history at the University of California, Los Angeles. He received many major prizes for his books on the history of Jews in the twentieth century.

In his books *Nazi Germany and the Jews: The Years of Persecution, 1933-1939* and *The Years of Extermination: Nazi Germany and the Jews, 1939–1945* (winner of the 2008 Pulitzer Prize for Nonfiction), Friedländer drew from newly available documents—such as local German police reports, films, personal recollections, as well as from his own experiences—producing an intimate picture of prewar Germany as grotesque and chilling under the veneer of an even more chilling normality. Most strikingly, Friedländer concludes that the largely middle-class, educated population of one of the world's most advanced nations "looked the other way" during the systematic removal of Jews from Germany's government, business, and cultural life in the pre-Holocaust years. In short, they viewed Hitler's anti-Jewish actions during a time of economic prosperity and growing international power as a "peripheral issue."

Friedländer documents how one anti-Jewish measure took place after another and the fate of each individual Jewish community in Europe. Thus, for example, in April 1933 alone, the Nazis declared a boycott of Jewish businesses, passed a law requiring non-Aryan civil servants to retire, and limited the number of Jewish students eligible to attend German universities. They compelled some two million state employees and tens of thousands of lawyers, doctors, students, and others to search for proof of Aryan ancestry and transformed tens of thousands of priests, pastors, town clerks, and archivists into investigators to vouch for blood purity.

According to Friedländer, Hitler's main goal in the late thirties was to force Jewish emigration by confiscating Jewish wealth, forcing Jews by law to sell their businesses, land, stocks, jewels, and artworks, thereby entirely destroying "any remaining possibility for Jewish life in Germany." Looting Jewish property on this scale was a substantial element of the twelve years of the Third Reich. Later, all the property of evacuated and murdered Jews was seized. Friedländer finds, however, no evidence of any plan for extermination prior to Germany's invasion of the Soviet Union. In all those years,

> not one social group, not one religious community, not one scholarly institution or professional association in Germany and throughout Europe declared its solidarity with the Jews...; to the contrary, many social constituencies, many power groups were directly involved in the expropriation of Jews and anxious, be it out of greed, for their wholesale disappearance. Thus *Nazi and*

anti-Jewish policies could unfold to their most extreme levels without the interference of any major countervailing interests.[36]

Friedländer collected layers of detail from the otherwise unremembered lives of people who ended up as corpses piled into the death pits. He is a world authority on the Shoah, as well as a survivor. "The goal of [conventional] historical knowledge," he writes, "is to domesticate disbelief." He states, instead, that disbelief is the only morally coherent starting point for thinking about what happened, a visceral response that should never be domesticated. He believes that the mass killings of Jews in the East—which were initially thought of simply as by-products of "the war of extermination and the destruction of 'Judeo-Bolshevism,'" were no different from the industrial genocide that followed. Friedländer's real purpose is not to lay bare the administrative machinery of the Holocaust, but to expose the failure of nerve at every level, and the profound *unwillingness* to confront it.

The Nazi state first achieved the isolation of millions of Jews from their neighbors through the ever-increasing weight of official vindictiveness. Jews were gradually restricted in their shopping hours, their schools, and their use of titles, telephones, cars, bicycles, and electrical appliances; they had to build their own air raid shelters, use their own cobblers, were denied fruit, gingerbread, chocolate, white bread, furs, and tobacco, and finally pets (which they couldn't even pass over to a neighbor, but were ordered to murder). Even so, when, in the East, the extermination began operating, Jews in the West could still live restricted lives for a while without a sense of immediate danger amid neighbors who, on a personal level, were sometimes sympathetic if unengaged. Friedländer's book stresses the collective timidity of so many with whom the reader can uncomfortably identify. Ordinary people may have been distressed by what they saw, but in the face of the state's

---

[36] Saul Friedländer, *Nazi Germany and the Jews: The Years of Persecution, 1933-1939* (New York: HarperCollins Publishers, 1997) and *The Years of Extermination: Nazi Germany and the Jews, 1939–1945* (New York: HarperCollins Publishers, 2007), xxi.

brutality and the success of its propaganda machine, they feared first for themselves.

According to Friedländer, while Hitler's personal obsession was the root cause of the Shoah, the course it took was only possible because of endemic European antisemitism. Friedländer charts chronologically the progress from administrative cruelties to the industrial mass murder of Auschwitz. His work helps explain the paralysis of Jews who were unable to accept what was happening until it was too late to escape and also how difficult it was for others to decide at what point to risk their own safety by taking a stand. Everyone went through a growing sense of disbelieving recognition. The few survivors lived subsequently in the shadow of the six million murdered. Some Jews were issued exemption stamps by the Nazis, but this only allowed people to save themselves at the expense of others and served to divide and demoralize the Jews via the institutions of Jewish council. Camp survivors were simply not believed.

Some occupied countries have better records about attempts to save Jews from the Nazi murderers than others. Belgium, Finland, Romania, Italy, Denmark, Bulgaria, and Hungary tried their best to stall or even obstruct deportations, while France, Switzerland, and Poland have particularly abominable records (not to mention Ukraine, Lithuania, and those other East European countries which actively participated in the murders). But even more distant countries famously returned ships with Jewish refugees back to Germany or Poland (Great Britain and the US, primarily). By the end of 1942, every nation knew—East and West—that the Jews were destined for complete extermination. Knowledge about the conditions and mass murders in concentration camps was also public by that time. The Vatican knew about it by early 1942. The pope did nothing and did not condemn the atrocities.[37] Europe turned from a home into the origin of a great exodus—there was no sense in staying anymore, even if one could save oneself. The Jews deported to concentration camps were subjected to inhuman treatment and humiliation,

---

[37]   Ibid., xxiii. Friedländer complains that the Vatican archives are still inaccessible to historians, as of writing this book.

which aimed at destroying their identities as human beings. Such extreme loss not only haunted survivors for the rest of their lives, but will also haunt future generations.

Friedländer's brilliant book of memoirs and essays *When Memory Comes* was published in 1978 in the US. It depicts another extreme form of exile as a personal loss of identity. Not only was he, as a young boy, forced to go through a sad separation from his parents, but he gradually lost a sense of who he was. This was forced upon him by the necessity to survive. He writes that he was denied his heritage and reality. In order to save his life, his parents kept his identity hidden from him and managed to place him in a Catholic boarding school. There, he became a devoted Catholic, living in a protected environment throughout the war, never knowing what was really going on, what had happened to his parents, or who he actually was.

When the war was over, a priest revealed the truth to him and a gradual awakening began. He was originally called Pavlíček, but to hide his Jewish associations his name was changed to Paul. After the war, he changed his name to Shaul and moved to Israel. The memoir is written in flashbacks to his former life in Prague and France. Thus, Pavlíček became Paul-Henri Ferland, then Shaul, and finally Saul. The book also shows how difficult it was for this assimilated and secular Jew to identify with the Jewish race. His Jewishness was purely negative, formed only from the outside and based on identification with his fellow sufferers. Being brought up Catholic, he had even taken on a subtle antisemitism. When offered to live with his grandmother in Sweden, he refused in order to continue his Catholic studies (he was planning to become a priest at that point). For a while, he lived with a Russian Polish Orthodox guardian. This gripping story of gradual awakening has become well known in the US, but still remains obscure in Friedländer's native land.

Friedländer's autobiographical story of loss of personal and national identity is a metaphor for a broader and systematic loss of identity imposed on the Jews by the events of the twentieth century in Europe—the gradual closing off of human living space, which became progressively hostile and unlivable.

10. Exile as Abandonment: Peter Weiss

The displacement, hostility, and lack of livable space peaks in a sense of abandonment due to extreme cruelty and lack of conscience that leads to senseless destruction and humiliation, typical of life in the concentration camps, where most Jews were forced to live in the war years. A painfully masterful and original description of this form of life can be found in the work of Peter Weiss (b. 1916 in Potsdam, d. 1982 in Stockholm).

Weiss was born in Germany. His father was a Hungarian Jewish German and his mother was a Christian. In 1934, his whole family emigrated to England. In 1937–38, he studied at the Art Academy in Prague. After the German occupation of the Sudetenland, Weiss's family emigrated to Sweden, while he moved to Switzerland. He did not stay long, and in early 1939 he joined the rest of his family in Sweden, where he lived until his death in 1982. Weiss's early life was characterized by wandering and a sense of homelessness, which had a profound effect on him.

His writing consists of short and intense Kafkaesque novels, with autobiographical components, as well as political plays and films. He established an international reputation with the Berlin production of *The Persecution and Assassination of Jean-Paul Marat as Performed by the Inmates of the Asylum of Charenton Under the Direction of the Marquis de Sade* (1963). In the play, he effectively uses the technique of the play within a play and juxtaposes two cruel historical personalities while asking about the need for revolution. The drama had great success in New York in Peter Brook's production and Weiss was heralded as the new Bertolt Brecht.

Weiss's next remarkable play *The Investigation* (1965) stages the Frankfurt trials (1963-65) of the Nazi criminals who worked at Auschwitz. A political drama, it is presented as "Oratoria with 11 cantos." It confronts the men who carried out the mass murders and tortures in the deathcamp. The play was performed in English translation by a Rwandan company in London in 2007 and drew parallels to that country's own genocide. Weiss received many prestigious international awards for his work.

The Investigation is an extensive play about the remarkable Frankfurt trials (known as the "second Auschwitz trial") that charged twenty-two defendants under German penal law for their roles in the Holocaust as mid- to low-level officials in the Auschwitz-Birkenau death camp. The defendants included Robert Mulka, adjutant to Rudolf Höss, the longest-standing commandant of the camp, who was turned over to Polish authorities in 1947 and hanged. Most of the senior leaders of the camp had already been tried in Cracow and sentenced to death. That trial became known as the "first Auschwitz trial." The defendants ranged from members of the SS, kapos, privileged prisoners responsible for the day-to-day control of camp internees and the selection process, during which, for example, children under fourteen were sent directly to the gas chambers upon arrival, along with mothers unwilling to part with their children.

In *The Investigation*, the audience experiences the feeling of exile as an encounter with extreme human cruelty and senseless destruction. Humanity vanishes, and there is an absolute absence of conscience. The human mind and heart literally shrink away from a world of such evil and a severe sense of abandonment results. The play very artfully and ingeniously shows the wide variety of tortures invented by people for people, as well as the impossibility of ever achieving justice. Weiss systematically concentrates on social rather than individual implications of his images of sickness, flagellation, and torture.

Weiss's aesthetics are clearly related to Brecht's. As Robert Cohen writes, "*The Investigation* subverts the notion of literature as a sphere distinct from other institutions in society. It insistently blurs the boundaries between reality and its representation, between documents and their interpretation, between authentic persons and stage characters. Interpretive strategies of his play need to confront this radical collapsing of traditional aesthetic categories."[38] This very subversion has been held against Weiss by many critics of Holocaust literature. Cohen continues, "But it is precisely the play's unrelenting recitation of atrocities which forces the reader/spectator to confront the essence of the Nazi state. *The Investigation* leaves us no choice but to try and understand a sphere inaccessible to most of us."[39]

There is, surprisingly, an affinity between the aesthetics of this play and *The Last Days of Mankind* by Karl Kraus in that both use documents and turn them into artistic discourse. Both works present enormous difficulty for performance because of their length and the detachment required from the viewer, as well as their depth and apocalyptic quality. Both are highly political and intrinsically critical of the political establishment. They constitute documentary dramas of sorts and are devastating in their conclusions. As different as they are, both have an expressionist character in that they use abstract symbols to stand for feelings. The multitudinous characters represent real persons of the periods represented. Reality speaks for itself. Both authors deny themselves artistic freedom in favor of depicting reality. While Kraus is, however, visionary and vast in his scope, Weiss focuses on a specific topic. Both dramas are stimulated by the deplorable events of WWI and WWII and are allegorical.

While Weiss's plays are still performed today, the peak of his success was his novel *Die Aesthetik des Widerstands* (*Aesthetics of Resistance*, 1975-81), considered one of the most significant examples of twentieth-century German literature. Weiss wrote in both Swedish and German. He is considered the ultimate exile, who lived in Germany only briefly. The defining places of his life were war-threatened Prague, England, and Sweden. He worked interchangeably as a painter, filmmaker, and writer and his methods range between surrealistic experiments and realistic autobiographical accounts.

[38] Robert Cohen, "The Political Aesthetics of Holocaust Literature: Peter Weiss's *The Investigation* and Its Critics," *History and Memory* 10, no. 2 (Fall 1998): 46.

[39] Ibid.: 48.

During the "second Auschwitz trial" in Frankfurt, referred to in Weiss's play, about 360 witnesses were called from nineteen countries, including around 210 survivors. Hessian attorney general Fritz Bauer was in charge of the trial, which came together almost by coincidence. Bauer was one of the few Germans who were seriously interested in pursuing Nazi criminals.

At this time, the far right still denied any gassing in Auschwitz and Bauer's trial managed to prove this definitively as a historical falsification. In fact, Helmut Kohl, later the chancellor of the FRG, was opposed to Bauer's intention to hold the trial and considered any judgment on National Socialism as "premature." Ultimately, a mere twenty-two of the 6,000 to 8,000 SS members involved in the camp administration were charged (only those who killed without orders to do so were found guilty). Information about the actions of those accused and their whereabouts had been in the possession of West German authorities since 1958, but action on their cases was delayed by jurisdictional disputes. The court's proceedings were largely public and served to bring many details of the Holocaust to the attention of the public in the Federal Republic of Germany and abroad. Six defendants were given life sentences and several others received the maximum prison sentences possible for the charges brought against them.

In 1977, an additional trial was held in Frankfurt for two former members of the SS for killing in a satellite camp. It is well known that the response of German courts to the Nazi regime and its monstrous crimes is one of the most disgraceful episodes in West German justice. Opposition to trials of this kind was widespread in the 1950s and '60s within Germany's legal and political elite. Many high-level war criminals, including the infamous Dr. Mengele, were given an opportunity to flee and hide in South America. The last commandant of Auschwitz, Richard Baer, declined to give any testimony during the preliminary investigation of the Frankfurt proceedings. He died in detention and all legal action against him was dropped.

The Frankfurt trial was valuable because it dealt with regular administrative members of the camp rather than those in charge, and thus gave a comprehensive picture of the seemingly banal daily routine and ghastly practices of the extermination and humiliation of the inmates. The trial served to politicize West German youth — young people began to think about their history and the deeds of their parents and grandparents.

Witnesses were required to describe their horrendous experiences in excruciating detail, while the defendants showed indifference and no regret or insight. A special hall eventually had to be built for the trial, which lasted twenty months, and 20,000 people attended the proceedings. Given that the trial was happening more than twenty years after the crimes were committed (a crime of its own), it was very challenging to prove beyond reasonable doubt that each of the defendants was individually complicit in the atrocities. This resulted in mild and inadequate sentences that bore no relation to the monstrous acts. Adolf Eichmann, who was convicted in Israel 1961, even considered himself a victim. His trial, however, stimulated interest in, and concern about, the Holocaust in the US.

The Investigation reads like a documentary of the Frankfurt Auschwitz trial. It lists the individual types of torture during daily life in Auschwitz. The work focuses on low-level officers, who insisted during the trials that they had not seen or participated in anything wrong. At best, they admitted occasionally contributing to what was going on—but only under duress, they claimed, or because it was required by the system. The witnesses are people, on the other hand, who personally recognize certain officers, doctors, political workers, and so on because they had a very close connection with them. Horrendous deeds of cruelty are described in a matter-of-fact way, as daily routine. The defendants are snotty and have no conscience whatsoever. The witnesses are referred to by numbers rather than names. This use of numbers creates a further atmosphere of impersonality and objectivity. The play is 30,000 words and lasts five hours. It has thirty characters. Its speeches are like arias.

The play is divided into cantos or songs: the song of the platform, the song of the camp, the song of the swing, the song of the possibility of survival, the song of the death of Lili Tofler, the song of SS Corporal Stark, the song of the "black" wall, the song of phenol, the song of the bunker block, the song of Zyklon B, the song of the fire ovens. Many of the songs have two or three parts. As Jürgen E. Schlunk observes, "Die Ermittlung [*The Investigation*—BV] carries distinct marks of its author's concern with Dante and his *Divine Comedy*. Structural and thematic connections with Dante's work can be found in Weiss's other plays such as *Mockinpott* or *Marat/Sade*."[40]

A lot of the witnessing happens in the first person singular, thus making the events very immediate and personal, as well as jarring and frightening. At the same time, the stark contrast between the narration of the witnesses and the accumulating knowledge of what they and their dead comrades went through is confronted with a total lack of feeling, compassion, empathy, personal responsibility, or even self-doubt on the part of the sneering and laughing accused. In fact, the defendants seem to feel that whatever they may have done wrong, they have already atoned for it. They are completely disconnected from reality. In fact, the estrangement technique used in the play, in which people end up mere figures and numbers, and the different torture places and techniques are personified by having a song ascribed to them, is a highly effective expressionistic device.

Abstractions come to life, while people are obliterated. The tortures are so devilish, it hurts to think of them as songs. At the same time, they present a theme to elaborate on in detail. What is especially powerful about this play are the small details, which the playwright is willing to unearth and explore so as not to forget a single thing. They also help to build up evidence against the defendants and evidence for posterity. There is little individuation in the play. The characters have equal roles and are almost interchangeable with each other. They only serve as vehicles for the documentation of what actually happened. The horrors and unbelievable circumstances are the true protagonists in this play. The lengthy topographical descriptions in *The Investigation* reproduce a sense of over-proximity to a place of death that nonetheless remains withdrawn from the imagination.

[40]   Jürgen E. Schlunk, "Auschwitz and Its Function in Peter Weiss' Search for Identity," *German Studies Review* 10, no. 1 (Feb. 1987): 20.

The structure of *The Investigation* parallels that of Dante's *Inferno*, in that it moves gradually toward the center of horror: from the ramp, to the inmates' barracks, the examination and torture rooms, the "black" wall where people were shot, the hospital where medical experiments were conducted, the bunker cells, the gas chambers, and finally to the ovens. The bare stage stresses the "non-place" or the emptied location and underlines the impossibility of identification with the place talked about. The human being goes into the extreme exile of losing his humaneness as well as his identity. Having also to face the absolute absence of conscience of the perpetrators results in a feeling of extreme abandonment.

11. Exile as Bearing Witness: Elie Wiesel

While Weiss's play is written as a mixture of documentary and fiction and is clearly a major avant-garde literary achievement portraying a loss of humanity and the absence of conscience in the face of it, there are a number of intimate, documentary accounts of the horrors of the Holocaust written by survivors. To name a few: the well-known Romanian Elie Wiesel, the Italian fighter for humanism Primo Levi; the tireless Galician Nazi hunter Simon Wiesenthal; the German-language Romanian poet Paul Celan; and the Hungarian Nobel Laureate Imre Kertész. They all belong to the genre of Holocaust literature, which portrays a form of exile as bearing witness in the most general sense of the word—yet each author brings their own special emphasis and insight. Each portrayal of the Holocaust is individual. There are as many Holocausts as there are people.

In order to bear witness, one must consciously remove oneself from being an actor or victim in life, to step aside, so to speak, in the interest of an objective representation of what happened. Wiesel, Levi, and Wiesenthal, whom we shall devote the next studies to, are not writers whose main ambition is to bring a new form of literary achievement into the world; rather, they are autobiographical, documentary writers, whose main goal is to share with the world their shattering experiences and interpretations. They are writers on a personal mission. They are the authors of a number of works on the topic, yet we shall focus only on selected ones.

The best known of these works is Elie Wiesel's (b. 1928 in Sighet, Romania, d. 2016 in New York City) famous memoir *Night*. The French original was published in 1958, after the first printing of the novel appeared in Yiddish in Buenos Aires under the title (*Un di velt hot geshvign*—And the world remained silent, 1954). The English translation, which followed four years later in the US, eventually sold ten million copies and was translated into thirty languages.

Wiesel was born in Romanian Transylvania. He received many prestigious prizes and honorary doctorates throughout his life and was awarded the Nobel Peace Price in 1986. He spent the latter part of his life (from 1955 onwards) in New York and Boston as a professor at the City University of New York and Boston University. He was a prolific political activist and a founder of the New York Human Rights Foundation. He is a foremost example of a major European literary and intellectual figure moving to the US and later on becoming erased from memory by the Communist regimes in Eastern Europe, whose countries moved from one harsh persecution and oppression to another even longer lasting.

Authors are often required to leave their mother tongue behind and adopt a new language. Jewish writers are the most frequent examples of this, as they are often the ones who have the courage to emigrate and start new lives in totally different countries. There, they are able to truly and fully express their talent and ideas and bring a new perspective to the world with an authenticity often lacking in national, narrowly conceived literatures.

Wiesel was the author of fifty-seven books, among which his memoir *Night*, describing his experiences as a prisoner in Auschwitz and Buchenwald has a special place. His family spoke Yiddish, but also German, Hungarian, and Romanian. Two of his sisters survived the war and were reunited with Wiesel at a French orphanage. His parents and younger sister perished. Wiesel's father, according to Wiesel, was beaten to death in front of his own eyes by a Nazi for suffering from dysentery, starvation, and exhaustion just a few months before the liberation of Buchenwald, where he and his son had ended up after a death march. After the war, Wiesel became a journalist and wrote for Israeli and French newspapers.

Night was originally turned down by fifteen publishers, even though it was proposed to them by the great French Catholic writer and journalist François Mauriac, a Nobel Prize winner for literature. Finally, the small firm Hill and Wang accepted the manuscript for publication. *Night* is a case study in how a book can create a genre, how a writer becomes an icon, and how the Holocaust was absorbed into the American experience. It was one of the first books to ask the question: "Where was God in Auschwitz?" This question does not, however, receive a satisfactory answer. Some critics of Wiesel's work feel that he even failed on this issue in order to appeal to the largely Christian world around him under the influence of his Catholic helper François Mauriac. They argue that he sublimated his rage at the perpetrators, and thus at God, for allowing such monstrosities to be committed. By casting himself as a suffering —but not raging— victim, he was able to be less offensive to his readers.[41]

A similar reading emerges from Naomi Seidman's comparison of the original Yiddish, Buenos Aires version of *Night* and the French one that achieved such fame: "What remains outside this proliferating discourse on the un-sayable is not what cannot be spoken but what cannot be spoken *in French*. And this is not the 'silence of the dead' but rather the scandal of the living, the scandal of Jewish rage and unwillingness to embody suffering and victimization."[42] According to Seidman, in order to reach a large audience, Wiesel sacrificed the anger of the Yiddish boy and became the personification of suffering silence acceptable to the Christian world.

Night is exquisitely constructed. Every sentence feels weighted and deliberate, every episode carefully chosen and delineated. It is also shockingly brief—a story as fundamentally brutal as this one would become grotesque if cluttered by embellishments. It is also devoid of rational explanations or cynicism. It reads as the innocent narration of a young boy who had no idea of what was coming. It compels the reader to become a witness to the unthinkable and absorb it inwardly. *Night* is not a novel and it is not exactly a memoir either. It has a hybrid form, which balances fidelity to events and literariness. The facts depicted are stranger than fiction. The English title itself was changed from the original Yiddish in

---

41 See Ron Rosenbaum, "Elie Wiesel's Secret," *Tablet*, September 28, 2018, https://www.tabletmag.com/sections/arts-letters/articles/elie-wiesels-secret.

42 Naomi Seidman, "Elie Wiesel and the Scandal of Jewish Rage," *Jewish Social Studies* 3, no. 1 (Autumn 1996): 8.

order to capture the darkness of the camp as well as the spiritual darkness of the world during and after WWII. The original version of the book was more than 800 pages, while the French publication was only 121 pages. Wiesel took out all the parts where he expressed his feelings about the Holocaust in the face of its denial, as well as any moralizing. His memoir is a genuine artistic achievement, and as such it is naturally not simply a literal description of facts but also austerely poetic. It simplifies the story into a kind of parable. It succeeds in individualizing the existential, depersonalized experience of the Holocaust, which made it possible for so many readers to start empathizing. In this way *Night* is like *The Diary of Anne Frank*,[43] which is easier to relate to, as it is the diary of a young girl in a chamber awaiting hell and thus does not force the reader to face the absolute horror of what succeeded.

The power of *Night* comes from the dramatic contrast between the thoughts and fears of the victims and their apathetic response. It offers not only a litany of the daily terrors, everyday perversions, and rampant sadism at Auschwitz and Buchenwald, but also an eloquent personal and philosophical treatise about what the Holocaust was, what it meant, and what its legacy is and will be. It is interesting to note that the book declines to address the sad fate of Wiesel's sisters and mother or what happened in the immediate aftermath of the liberation. In any case, it is in part thanks to this book that Auschwitz has become more than just a place: it has become shorthand for the Shoah, a common metaphor for uncommon evil, an almost platitudinous sign for hell on earth.

The book clearly invites many questions. In the first place, it questions whether or not the Enlightenment came to an end with the Shoah. Was it the result of totalitarianism of mass society, where the individual has become depersonalized, colonized, and

---

[43] First published in Amsterdam, the Netherlands, in Dutch in 1947, the English translation—*Anne Frank: The Diary of a Young Girl*, trans. Valentine Mitchell (New York: Doubleday & Company, 1952) received widespread critical and popular attention. It was translated into sixty languages.

alienated by huge forces that escape our understanding and control? Could anything have been done to prevent the genocide? Did the perpetrators have options or were they forced to simply follow orders? Similar questions were asked at the end of the Communist era and are still debated today. Is there personal responsibility? What is its extent? Is the victim to be blamed? Could the Jews foresee what was coming and could they have prevented it by an escape? Who are we obliged to help? It has been proven that indifference is equal to complicity, yet there are genocides happening all over the world today and we remain largely indifferent to them as long as they do not affect us personally.

The US often positions itself as the protector of law and security around the world, but it does not have a consistent policy in punishing perpetrators of genocide or an ability to prevent the horrors of lawlessness. Genocide and war crimes are clearly defined nowadays, but responses to them remain largely ineffective.

I feel that we must study what produces the authoritarian personality and what produces prejudice. We have known for a long time that prejudice against Jews is based predominantly on their being presented as killers of Jesus Christ, as Zionist conspirators who want to take over the world (as purported in the fake document *The Protocols of the Elders of Zion*), as contaminators of pure Aryan blood, as the chosen nation, and so forth. Yet Jews are not the only ones currently being subjected to extermination.

The mechanization of the complete destruction of an entire race organized and carried out by a state shows how reason is something that can be abused in a vile way. It can be twisted and then used to defend inhumanity. The Soviet gulags and the Nazi camps had many similarities. According to Primo Levi, the death rate in the Gulags was about thirty percent, while in the Nazi camps it was ninety to ninety-eight percent. The aim of the death camps was to annihilate an entire race, not only the extermination of individuals opposing a certain ideology or state form. So there is both a great similarity as well as a difference between the two systems. Writers bearing personal witness have had a great impact helping people attempt to understand something that is almost unimaginable.

Elie Wiesel created a purpose for his life as a survivor:

> My universe is the universe of the survivor. Writing is a duty for me as a survivor. I entered literature through silence; I seek the role of witness, and I am duty bound to justify each moment of my life as a survivor. Not to transmit my experience is to betray that experience. Words can never express the inexpressible; language is finally inadequate, but we do know of the beauty of literature. We must give truth a name, force man to look. The fear that man will forget, that I will forget, that is my obsession. Literature is the presence of the absence. Since I live, I must be faithful to the memory. Though I want to celebrate the sun, to sing of love, I must be the emissary of the dead, even though the role is painful.[44]

Bearing witness prevents humanity from forgetting and this must not be left undone, according to Elie Wiesel.

Marie Cedars writes that "silence is the language of Wiesel's first book, *Night*, as it documents the camp experience that killed his faith 'forever.'" Such is the claim in her article from 1986. She continues: "Its neutral tone is the language of the witness. Silence as a mood, silence as a mysterious presence, remains in Wiesel's books, even while he moves from despair to affirmation of literature and life and as he continues to probe the unanswered questions of human cruelty and God's silence."[45]

Peter Manseau recapitulates the differences between the Wiesel's original Yiddish book, written immediately at the end of the Holocaust, and the translation of *Night* presented to the world more than a decade later. He believes that rather than suppress his Jewish rage (as claimed by Seidman), Wiesel imposes "a theological

---

[44] Heidi Ann Walker, and Elie Wiesel, "Why and How I Write: An Interview with Elie Wiesel," *Journal of Education* 162, no. 2 (Spring 1980): 58.

[45] Marie M. Cedars, review of *Against Silence: The Voice and Vision of Elie Wiesel*, by Irwing Abrahamson, *Cross Currents* 36, no. 3 (Fall 1986): 258-9.

frame on the story."[46] He goes on: "Wiesel has created a mouthpiece for his theology. It is a unique Holocaust theology, a theology of questions without answers: one that equates knowledge of the depths of man's depravity with knowledge of the heights of man's wisdom." Thus, the main message of the book is shifted from man's depravity to God's silence interpreted as wisdom. Manseau believes that this is shortchanging the meaning that can be found in the excruciating experience: "If we continue to speak of atrocity in religious terms we will never take full responsibility for it. And so we will never learn. And so it will continue to be denied. And so it will happen again."[47]

Another way in which the pain of what happened has been circumvented is by predominantly focusing on children as survivors or witnesses of the Holocaust. Mark Anderson proposes that this "allowed for mainstream, Christian identification with the Jewish victims, thus facilitating a crucial breakthrough in public recognition of the Jewish tragedy. But it also depoliticized and sacralized the Holocaust, filed off the rough edges of the Jewish protagonists, and sought reconciliation rather than confrontation with the gentile world that had assisted Hitler's genocidal plan by remaining silent."[48]

The question remains as to whether Wiesel's masterpiece can continue to have an effect on future generations, those who will be far removed from the historical environment he described.

---

[46]   Peter Manseau, "Revising *Night*: Elie Wiesel and the Hazards of Holocaust Theology," *Cross Currents* 56, no. 3 (Fall 2006): 396.

[47]   Ibid.: 399.

[48]   Mark M. Anderson, "The Child Victim as Witness to the Holocaust: An American Story?," *Jewish Social Studies* 14, no. 1 (Fall 2007), pp. 1–22.

12. Exile as Dehumanization: Primo Levi

Among those bearing witness, the Italian chemist and writer Primo Levi (b. 1919 in Turin, d. 1987 in Turin) stands out due to his thorough, sober, and analytical approach to the Holocaust. He was the author of many books, novels, collections of short stories, essays, and poems. His best-known works include *If This is a Man* (1947; US title, *Survival in Auschwitz*, 1959), his account of the year he spent as a prisoner in the Auschwitz concentration camp, *The Truce* (1963), *The Periodic Table* (1975), which linked Holocaust stories to the elements, and *The Drowned and the Saved* (1986).

Levi became "the other" prominent voice in American Holocaust discourse during the 1980s. There is a huge body of literature comparing Primo Levi and Elie Wiesel. Of all Holocaust survivors, these two have become the most important voices, especially in the US, as their works were frequently written about in the *New York Times Book Review*, *Publishers Weekly*, the *Hudson Review*, *World Literature Today*, *Newsweek*, the *Wall Street Journal*, *Time*, *The Nation*, the *New Republic*, the *Chicago Tribune*, the *Chicago Sun-Times Book Review*, *Atlantic Monthly*, the *LA Times Book Review*, *Vanity Fair*, and other influential media. They have also been widely discussed by American academics and featured in Jewish and Holocaust courses. Paradoxically, they are not so well known in Central and Eastern Europe due to those areas' cultural insulation during the Communist period.

Levi had an urgent concern to communicate his experiences during the Holocaust to a broader public, as well as to future generations, and judging from his reception both in his native Italy and particularly in the US, we can say he succeeded. Levi suffered, however, for the rest of his postwar life from a feeling of not having been heard, especially by the Germans, at whom his accounts were pointedly directed. There are many important lessons to be derived from his thoughtful and insightful accounts. He was a scientist and his autobiographical books carry the clear stamp of a precise mind. As Alvin Rosenfeld puts it in his well-known book comparing Elie Wiesel's *Night* and Primo Levi's *Survival in Auschwitz*, "[g]rounded in a humane intelligence and persistently curious and observant, . . . [Levi] turned toward whatever remains of the human race after it has been pummeled and befouled by the crimes of the camp."[49] Levi's first book on this topic was written in 1946 and in 1987 he ended his life by jumping from the third story of his apartment building.

Levi comes from a very different background than Elie Wiesel. He is the prototype of the assimilated and acculturated European Jew, not an Orthodox Jew from a shtetl. During Mussolini's rule in Italy, Jews were able to hold public positions and were prominent in literature, science, and politics. While Catholicism was established as the state religion, other religions had the status of "tolerated cults." The situation changed radically as a result of the 1940 alliance with Hitler's Germany. Italian Jews lost their basic civil rights, positions in public office, as well as their assets. Their books were prohibited; Jewish writers could no longer publish in magazines owned by Aryans. Jewish students who had begun courses of study were permitted to continue, but new Jewish students were barred from entering universities.

Levi matriculated a year earlier than scheduled, enabling him to finish with a degree, but he could no longer secure a suitable position after graduation. Eventually, he was forced to escape into the mountains where he joined the partisan resistance. He was captured and arrested at the end of 1943 and sent into the internment camp Fossoli. As long as the camp was under the control of the Italian Social Republic, he was not harmed. According to his descriptions, life in the camp was rather humane. Once Fossoli was taken over by the Germans, however, transfers to Poland began. In February 1944, Levi was on the second transfer, and spent eleven months in Auschwitz before its liberation by the Red Army in January 1945.

---

[49] Alvin H. Rosenfeld, *A Double Dying: Reflections on Holocaust Literature* (Bloomington: Indiana University Press, 1980), 56.

Of the 650 Jews on his transport, Levi was one of only twenty to survive. The average survival rate was three months.

Levi is extremely specific about the reasons why he managed to survive. His qualification as a chemist proved useful in the camp, making it possible to avoid hard labor in freezing temperatures; his knowledge of German helped, as well as his access to materials that he was able to steal and exchange for extra food. He was further saved by falling ill at an opportune time, just before liberation, when the Germans sent all the remaining prisoners in the camp on a death march, except the gravely ill. Levi stresses the fact that one could only survive in a German camp on the basis of luck or on the basis of gaining privileges at the expense of others. He has tremendous respect for those who perished and he stresses that the survivors were those who did not reach the depths of hell. The ones who did reach the depths of hell were called *Muslims*. They were those whose sense of dignity and humanity, as well as the will to live, was completely destroyed. In Levi's later writings (*The Truce*, for instance), he also describes his long and arduous journey home, which took almost a year of traveling through Poland, Belarus, Ukraine, Romania, Austria, and Germany.

In the Soviet Union, his early works were not accepted by censors as they portray Soviet soldiers as slovenly and disorderly rather than heroic. In Israel, a country partly formed by Holocaust survivors, many of his works were not translated and published until after his death, perhaps due to his criticism of the country's political direction.

Apart from his witnessing of the systematic dehumanization of the Jews in concentration camps, Levi's concept of exile (and he considers displacement and forced migration as such) includes the issue of shame and guilt. The inhabitants of the camps were plagued by shame for what their fellow human beings were doing to them and by the extent to which their captors had reduced their lives to a condition of animality and humiliation. Those who survived were plagued by a sense of guilt for both being unable to avoid this or by surviving while their friends and family members died, or even by surviving in place of another. Other refugees, who were not necessarily tortured by first hand memories of concentration camps, interestingly, carry similar feelings, even if perhaps not as acutely.

In *The Drowned and the Saved*, Levi openly writes that

the saved of the Lager were not the best, those predestined to do good, the bearers of a message: what I have seen and lived proved the exact contrary. Preferably the worst survived, the selfish, the violent, the insensitive, the collaborators of the "grey zone", the spies. It was not a certain rule (there were none, nor are there certain rules in human matters), but it was nevertheless a rule. I felt innocent, yes, but enrolled among the saved and therefore in permanent search of a justification in my own eyes and those of others. The worst survived, that is, the fittest, the best all died."[50]

On a lesser level, the feeling of guilt of émigrés from the Communist countries was similar. They often felt ashamed of having a better life than those who remained behind the Iron Curtain.

Levi says:

I must repeat: we, the survivors, are not the true witnesses. This is an uncomfortable notion, of which I have become conscious little by little, reading the memoirs of others and reading mine at a distance of years. We survivors are not only an exiguous but also an anomalous minority: we are those who by their prevarications or abilities of good luck did not touch bottom. Those who did so, those who saw the Gorgon, have not returned to tell about it or have returned mute, but they are the "Muslims," the submerged, the complete witnesses, the ones whose deposition would have a general significance.[51]

Further, Levi quotes Solzhenitsyn, who expresses a similar opinion. This suggests another understanding of exile as the survival of the fittest (not the best). Under the given circumstances, the exceptional, living ones, absurdly, are the outcasts of death.

Levi is thus exceptional for not attributing a false meaning to his survival: that would give a special reason for it and would thus, as a consequence, give a false meaning to the death and suffering of

---

[50]   Primo Levi, *The Drowned and the Saved*, trans. Raymond Rosenthal (New York: Summit Books; Simon & Schuster, 1988), 82.

[51]   Ibid., 83–84.

the majority. As a race, Jews have experienced an exile during this period of time, which can be described as an absolute condemnation in the name of eradication. This, accompanied by complete dehumanization is beyond human comprehension, and thus, many Jews have not recovered from the trauma. For Levi, comprehending the incomprehensible became a life challenge. He refused to ultimately measure humanity's character by Auschwitz, instead considering it an anomaly in order to preserve a measure of dignity for mankind. As Joseph Farrell puts it, his "deep reverence for humanity and for the value of life, even *in extremis*, remained intact."[52]

The issue of the difficulty in communicating is another prominent feature of exile, which again in the concentration camp situation became extreme. Not only were people thrown among others of different language groups, but their survival depended on their ability to understand the requirements of their torturers. Communication, or the lack thereof, is thus described in Levi as a matter of life and death. In the face of the first trauma experienced by the condemned, namely the forced departure toward the unknown, this lack of communication becomes more than critical and it is a general issue faced by refugees in general.

Levi further gives a detailed description of the useless violence that characterized the Nazi handling of Jews and concludes that the main purpose of it consisted in the degradation of the victims in order to cleanse the conscience of the perpetrators.[53] He insists on the Holocaust having nothing to do with the war per se, but rather with purposeful brutalization and dehumanization, and, in this, he sees its historical uniqueness. Neither the Holocaust nor the systematic attack on the Jews were new, Levi argues,

> since, deplorably, such murderous pogroms had been known before in European history; but the specifically Nazi program of "demolishing the human" was new. It was this outrage that

[52] Joseph Farrell, "The Humanity and Humanism of Primo Levi," in *Answering Auschwitz: Primo Levi's Science and Humanism after the Fall*, ed. Stanislao G. Pugliese (New York: Fordham University Press, 2011), 102.

[53] Levi, *The Drowned and the Saved*, 126.

he believed, and indeed stated explicitly, had no precedent in history. He rejected the lazy notion that such degradation was an accidental side effect of Nazi brutality, insisting that it required to be seen as an intrinsic part of the project, "a precise objective," or "act of will."[54]

Levi also devotes chapters to the problems of the intellectual in Auschwitz, to stereotypes, and to German responses to his work. His ruthless analysis of the roots and consequences of the evil he encountered brings him gradually to the conclusion that it is omnipresent in mankind and will be repeated.[55]

After the war, Levi was horrified when he encountered people who tried to describe the camps as less horrific than they were in reality, that is, Holocaust deniers—as well as the continued indifference of the "passive" participants of the crimes committed. Even though his death left some doubts as to whether it was a suicide, his doctor ruled it as such. His fellow traveler Elie Wiesel, concluded that Levi died in Auschwitz—but forty years later.

Rothberg and Druker describe the role of the two prominent Holocaust witnesses, Wiesel and Levi, in the following way:

> Wiesel will always be the more well-known figure, but his fame will come at the expense of a certain respect among the more "serious" academics (although, to be sure, there is an enormous academic industry dedicated to his work, which remains among the most frequently taught in schools and universities); Levi, on the other hand, will not reach the same mass audience as Wiesel, but he will come to be the favorite of the American intellectual class. Levi will remain linked with sober historiography and documentary writing—with Enlightenment rationality— while Wiesel will continue to have a reputation as an emotive, mythologizing prophet.[56]

---

54 Farrell, "The Humanity and Humanism of Primo Levi": 88–89.

55 See Tzvetan Todorov, "Ten Years Without Primo Levi," *Salmagundi*, nos. 116/117 (Fall/Winter 1997): 16.

56 Michael Rothberg, and Jonathan Druker, "A Secular Alternative: Primo Levi's Place in American Holocaust Discourse," *Shofar* 28, no. 1 (Fall 2009): 120.

13. Exile as an Awakening of Consciousness: Jiří Weil, Ladislav Fuks, Arnošt Lustig

Having discussed three writers of the Holocaust who are famous in the West, let us now turn to some less prominent authors who wrote in Czech. Weiss wrote in German, Wiesel became well known after the French edition of *Night,* and Levi wrote in Italian, but was translated into English by Raymond Rosenthal and widely read.

Jiří Weil, Ladislav Fuks, and Arnošt Lustig, on the other hand, all wrote in Czech and only Lustig was widely published in English because of his late exile to the US after 1968 and because some of his works were turned into films. These writers present a very different take on the lives of Jews during WWII. The Czech sensibility is unique. It contains aspects of absurdity and Surrealism, twisted humor and lyricism, individualism, eroticism, and profundity. It is aesthetic rather than strictly rational.

Jiří Weil, an outstanding Czech Jewish author (b. 1900 in Praskolesy, d. 1959 in Prague) wrote among other things a masterful little novel titled *A Life with Star* (1949), which in a very direct and unexpected way takes on the issue of how to create meaning in the absolutely absurd world into which the hero is thrown. Weil was an avant-garde artist and member of Devětsil (an influential avant-garde association of artists founded in 1920 in Prague), an award-winning novelist, a literary translator, a journalist, and a curator. He was one of the first to write about the Soviet purges in a novel, the very first writer to set a novel in a Gulag, and among the first writers (together with Arnošt Lustig and Ladislav Fuks) to consider the fate of the Czech Jews in WWII.

A pupil of the prominent critic F. X. Šalda, Weil studied philosophy and comparative literature at Charles University,

Prague, and was one of the first translators of contemporary Russian literature into Czech (Pasternak, Mayakovsky, Tsvetaeva). He worked in Russia as a journalist in the 1930s, but after the assassination of Kirov, he was thrown out of the Communist Party and exiled to Central Asia.[57] He returned to Prague in 1935 and published a novel about the Soviet purges in 1937. During the Nazi occupation, he escaped deportation to the Terezín (Theresienstadt) ghetto by staging his own death and going into hiding until the end of the war.

His best-known work *Life with a Star* was published just after the 1948 Communist February Putsch in Czechoslovakia and thus received a poor reception, as it was labeled by the new authorities as decadent, existentialist, highly subjective, the "product of a cowardly culture" and banned. He was only readmitted into the Writers' Union after the death of Klement Gottwald.[58]

He was introduced to American readers by Philip Roth and today he is considered a major Czech writer. Critics agree that his is one of the most outstanding works about the Holocaust and the fate of individual Jews.

Weil never mentions the words "Jew," "German," or "Nazi" in the whole book, yet, and perhaps because of it, he produces a sense of authenticity, as well as urgency and timelessness. He further switches between impersonal and objective narration and subjective narration, which gives the narrator agency with regard to reality.[59]

---

[57]   Sergei Mironovich Kirov, First Secretary of the central committee of the Azerbaijani Communist Party and a personal friend of Joseph Stalin. He rose through the ranks of the Communist Party of the Soviet Union to become head of the party in Leningrad and a member of the Politburo. He was assassinated in 1934. His death was later used as a pretext to escalate political repression in the Soviet Union and Great Purge that followed. Weil's persecution was part of the aftermath of his death.

[58]   Klement Gottwald was the first Communist president of Czechoslovakia. During his rule the most deadly purges were carried out. He died only several days after Stalin in 1953.

[59]   See also, Eva Štědroňová, "Dialektika umělecké metody a reality v díle Jiřího Weila," *Česká literatura* 38, no. 2 (1990): 130.

The novel describes the existence of a solitary Jew, Josef Roubíček living in Prague during the German occupation. He lives without an income, in hunger and cold, ostracized and degraded, and tries to get through life without getting murdered. He is bombarded by daily prohibitions on anything and everything and by the daily fear of being called for deportation, which he knows is a journey to death. He is an orphan who was brought up by abusive relatives, which has resulted in an anxious and cowardly attitude to life. In his mind, he is constantly having conversations with Růžena, his married lover, who is no longer around, as she has emigrated with her husband.

Roubíček, however, is too afraid to follow suit, as many of his compatriots also were. It is scary and difficult to move to a strange country and he cannot overcome his fear. He is simply forced into an inner exile of the most gruesome and absurd kind. One of his acquaintances commits suicide in order to improve his daughter's life: he believes her life will be easier with him gone, as she is a child of mixed marriage. His fellow Jews, who are wealthier than him, are easier targets for the Nazis, as robbing the Jews is their first and foremost goal. Roubíček's friends and neighbors check their future possessions before their Jewish acquaintances are deported, as they are virtually already dead.

The best part of Roubíček's life takes place at a cemetery, where he cultivates some vegetables in order to survive. His best friend is a stray cat, who he secretly adopts, as Jews are not allowed to have pets and are even ordered to kill them. He has to pretend the cat is actually just a stray, even though he becomes his bed and table companion. The cat is eventually shot by the Nazis for sport and eaten by his neighbors, while Josef is forced to pretend to have no feelings about the matter.

He eventually realizes, though, how reduced and thwarted his life has become purely due to his own fear of death. This creates a major personal breakthrough for him after a long fear-based existence. He decides against joining a transport when called and goes into hiding. We do not find out anything about his further fate, but it is implied that he has found a path toward a meaningful life through his epiphany. He understands now that should he die, he will be actually free. The cemetery appears as a peaceful place; the dead are safe from the Nazis.

People around Josef die not only in an inhuman way, but also in an absurd way, exhausted and numbed by waiting for death and desperately trying to defend themselves against the horrendous conditions they are subjected to. They die inside by scheming how to save this or that tiny part of their existence or possessions. Their martyrdom becomes an absurd martyrdom and death an absurd death. But Josef also understands that the Jews absurdly helping the enemy to dig their own graves is due to their holding onto hope. Hope is thus a major source of degradation. Josef's victory over himself is a victory over hope. The internal exile he has condemned himself to, because of his fear of external exile, is transformed into a concept of exile as abandoning hope, in a positive sense, into understanding life as transcending death.

Ladislav Fuks (b. 1923 in Prague, d. 1994 in Prague), on the other hand, who wrote several important novels about the periods of the Holocaust and Communist regime—for example, *Mr. Theodor Mundstock* (1963), *Variation on the Dark String* (1966), *The Burner of the Corpses* (1967, made into a famous film by Juraj Herz in 1968), and *Of Mice and Mooshaber* (1970)—turns the same topics into Surrealist dreamlike nightmares. His obsession with the topic of Jewish persecution during the Nazi occupation of Czechoslovakia, to which his best novels refer, is interesting also because he himself was not a Jew. He was, however, a homosexual and thus subject to a very similar kind of ostracism as Jews. He makes his heroes escape into an unreal, dreamlike world, where their circumstances and their reactions to these circumstances are multiplied and exaggerated. The reader is confronted with a nightmarish experience, which forces them to receive the book's message on a subconscious level. The reader might also be more willing to face up to the contents of the novels because they seem "unreal."

Fuks explicitly uses a method of literary mystification.[60] He intentionally thwarts his narrative, filling it with words, themes,

---

[60]   See Ladislava Lederbuchová, "Ladislav Fuks a literární mystifikace," *Česká literatura* 34, no. 3 (1986): 232–244.

motives, and stories that appear to have one meaning, but later on turn out to mean something completely different. His early works deal with the Holocaust in very personal and ingenious ways. *The Burner of the Corpses* has been turned into a well-known Czech New Wave film. His later works are more abstract, and are harder for readers to decipher.

His books are not allegories, as they might seem, but complicated structures of meaning that interact on many planes. The protagonist of *Of Mice and Mooshaber*, for example, appears as an enigmatic and abused old woman throughout the novel. She is suspected of using rat poison on children, but at the end she turns into a powerful aristocrat who was in disguise the whole time. The reader is thus forced to suddenly reevaluate the whole semantic structure of the book and the reality they have been exposed to.

Unfortunately, Ladislav Fuks was among those that after the Soviet invasion in 1968 was willing to reconcile with the regime rather than stand up to it. His strongest works, then, are those written in the 1960s about the German occupation.

Other significant Jewish authors coming from Czechoslovakia dealt with exile and extreme conditions in a much lighter way. Arnošt Lustig (b. 1926 in Prague, d. 2011 in Prague) is probably the most renowned of the Czech Jewish authors. His many novels and stories focus primarily on the fate of Jews in the Holocaust. He views the Jews as the embodiment of the general human problem of the twentieth century, namely the conflict between destructive and impersonal political power and the individual.

The theme of the awakening of individual human consciousness is the predominant subject of Lustig's works. His protagonists are often young women. His works achieved success even during the Communist era, as they offered a fresh perspective by removing themselves from the prescribed ideological fiction of the time. His major achievement is his presentation of inhuman conditions as an everyday matter. In this sense, his protagonists are ordinary.

This denial of hero status was another revolutionary act during the Communist period. Despite Lustig's popularity and the relative approbation he received in the 1960s, he decided to emigrate to America after the Soviet occupation in 1968, where he achieved success as a professor of literature at the American University in Washington D.C., as well as a writer and filmmaker.

His road to success in America, however, was not easy. His first books, including the novel *The Prayer for Katarina Horowitzova* (1964), which was made into a successful film later on, first received a fairly negative reception.[61] It might be Lustig's ingenious idea of focusing on a group of rich American Jews, portrayed in a rather negative light that made the novel unappealing to critics. Yet it was precisely this that made it possible for the novel to get published and appreciated in Communist Czechoslovakia in the 1960s. It also gives the book a wider perspective. While showing the clear amorality and ruthlessness of the Germans, the novel at the same time does not idealize the Nazis' victims or paint a black-and-white picture. The reader follows the story with a curious eye, rather than with mere disgust for the Germans. It is the one novel by Lustig that has an unambiguous heroine in the person of the young Polish dancer Katarina. She is presented as pure, wholesome, and strong, capable of resistance and a conscious stance that puts everybody else to shame.

On the whole, however, Lustig's work is characterized by its avoidance of heroic topics and its refusal to celebrate the Czech resistance. He chose mostly very young people for his protagonists and, in his later works, especially young girls, who sell their bodies to improve their lives in the concentration camps.

In conclusion, I would like to briefly mention a few other major Czech writers who addressed the idea of Jews as outcasts.

Viktor Fischl (Avigdor Dagan) (b. 1912 in Hradec Králové, d. in Israeli exile in 2006) fled to Israel at the beginning of WWII to flee from the Nazi terror. He belongs among the most important exiled writers who were, at the time, interested in what was happening to European Jews. He worked for many years as an Israeli diplomat. His most famous novel *Dvorní šašci* (Court jester, 1990) describes the fate of a Jew who has survived a concentration camp due to his physical handicap and his role as an entertainer.

---

[61] Abraham Rothberg, review of *A Prayer for Katerina Horovitzova*, by Arnost Lustig, *Southwest Review* 59, no. 1 (Winter 1974): 87–89.

Jan Otčenášek (b. 1924 in Prague, d. 1979 in Prague) is a Czech non-Jewish writer famous for his novel *Romeo, Juliet, and Darkness* (1958) about the young love between a Jewish girl in hiding and a Czech student during the German occupation. The novel was made into a successful film. The setting and outcome are very similar to Anne Frank's—the innocence of youth violated by an ugly and pitiless world.

Norbert Frýd (b. 1913 in České Budějovice, d. 1976 in Prague) is the author of *Box of Lives* (1956), a novel based on his own experiences in German concentration camps.

Ladislav Grosman (b. 1921 in Humenné, Slovakia, d. 1981 in Tel Aviv), is a Slovak Jewish author who later wrote in Czech and became world famous because of his screenplay for the film *Shop on Main Street* (1965), which was directed by Jánoš Kádár and Elmar Klos. He emigrated to Israel after the Soviet invasion of 1968.

The topic of the persecution of the Jews during the German occupation described by Czech-Jewish authors was readily accepted during the Communist regime, even if it did not fit the strict demands of Socialist Realism, as it also served to capture something of the suffering of the Czechs and Slovaks under the Nazis. The awakening of consciousness, which sometimes takes the form of a subtle shift in perception, sometimes a psychological breakthrough under extreme duress and isolation (see Weil, Lustig, and Fuks), is the thread that unifies these writings

14. Exile as a Feeling of Meaninglessness: Egon Hostovský

An entirely different characteristic of the human mind is explored by the well-known Czech Jewish author and émigré Egon Hostovský (b. 1908 in Hronov, Czech Republic, d. 1973 in Montclair, New Jersey). Hostovský went into exile twice. First in 1939 to escape the Nazis; the second time in 1948 to escape the Communists. On both occasions he ended up in the United States, where he lived for thirty years until he died in 1973. His family perished in Hitler's concentration camps.

Hostovský was a very prolific and quite established author of philosophical, social, and psychological novels already before WWII. He chose external exile consciously because of his dedication to literature, which he could pursue in Czechoslovakia under the Communist regime only in an adulterated form. This decision was very brave, but at the same time costly, as he lived in double exile — in a culture foreign to his own and, essentially, without readers. His exile thus has a very different character from the inner exile or short-term concentration camp exile described in the studies above.

Hostovský continued to write in Czech in America and published his novels in translation. They are mainly about the lives of exiles in the States. His work, however, is of a universal, philosophical type. He is admired for his humanism and psychological observation. Even though he had connections in diplomatic circles, was befriended by the most prominent Czech writers, as well as writers like Graham Green, and despite having a family that joined him, his life in American exile was torture to him. Yet he insisted on continuing with it. He put it succinctly to A. Liehm in his last interview (1974): "What's the use of language if there's no freedom?

Who knows, perhaps the very fact of my exile and the irreparable loss of my original roots, of my native land, inspired me to do the kind of work which can only be done in exile."[62] The predicament of exile is well expressed in the same interview by great Czech author Pavel Kohout: "For people like us, each choice is wrong and ridiculous in its own way. But that's what's typical of the situation in which we've found ourselves or into which we've been thrust."[63] Liehm comments: "Perhaps this is the biggest and most tragic problem, bigger than exile itself: the writer outside his own country and away from its language, in which he continues to write."[64]

Hostovský's themes are very broad. His concern is human nature, the mind, and the fate of modern man under the pressure of the state and its institutions. If we were to interpret the meaning of exile in his works, we could say that, by and large, exile for Hostovský is banishment and solitude. These experiences, so particularly and painfully known to European Jews, are nevertheless those of twentieth-century man as a whole. That is why Hostovský's novels always have a transcendent quality and make a statement about the human predicament in general.

His heroes are often people who are oppressed by modern society, buried beneath mechanized and meaningless tasks which are invariably put above the interests of the individual. The individual is ultimately crushed by superior forces. Looking for meaning is thus Hostovský's main task. His characters are often lost in the labyrinth of their alienating worlds. The reason for this is partly because they do not see the world as objectively good or bad; their only perspective on it is through their own values. At the same time, they are manipulated by the social systems against which they have no chance of winning and whose motives are base.

Society and its institutions keep man in a frenzy of self-forgetting and maddening activity. People get swept into absurd struggles for

---

[62] A. J. Liehm, "Egon Hostovský: A Last Conversation," *Canadian Slavonic Papers* 16, no. 4 (Winter 1974): 548.

[63] Ibid.: 550.

[64] Ibid.: 560.

absolute power and in vain try to return to feelings of solidarity with each other. But it is difficult for them to find any meaningful purpose. Exile in Hostovský's work is the hopelessness caused by the individual's feeling that life is meaningless. Oppressive governments and institutions, being policed in various ways, being oppressed by technology, alienation, forced conformity—all contribute to this feeling of meaninglessness.

This state of mind, so common among actual refugees, can be found among intelligent people in modern civilization everywhere. The Jewish refugee is thus emblematic of modern man. Even though Hostovský is only meagerly recognized in his home country, where he was proscribed for decades as an émigré, and in his adopted country America, where he was poorly understood and marginalized, his extensive work contributes to twentieth-century thinking about man's desperate struggle to find the self-knowledge and values that would create a world he could actually truly belong to. Hostovský's writing is clearly a continuation of Kafka's take on the world. Their heroes are people who are attempting to make sense of their solitary existence in an alienating world. The fact that Kafka was not compelled to leave his native country, while political circumstances forced exile upon Hostovský, does not change the fact that the two writers' heroes share a similarity in their deep emotional quality.

15. Exile as Transformation and a Will to Meaning: Viktor Frankl, Simon Wiesenthal

For a few outstanding writers, scholars, and individuals, exile turns into a personal transformation. A scholarly way of addressing the extreme inhumanity of the world is found in the work of the Viennese psychologist Viktor Frankl (b. 1905 in Vienna, d. 1997 in Vienna). His book *Man's Search for Meaning* (1946) has become a bestseller due to its response to the postwar generation's need to come to terms with a world forever changed.

Frankl chose to stay with his parents in Vienna, even though he had a visa to escape to the US, and thus went through the frightening experiences of Theresienstadt, Auschwitz, and Dachau, where most of his family died. The only survivor was his sister Stella, who emigrated to Australia after the war.

Unlike Freud, Frankl came to the conclusion that neurosis arises from the individual's failure to find meaning and a sense of responsibility for their existence, rather than a question of sexual instincts and repressions. He was the founder of the Third Viennese School of Psychotherapy. The Second School was formed by Alfred Adler (b. in Vienna in 1870, d. 1937 in Aberdeen, Scotland), a Viennese Jew who had to close his clinics (even though he converted to Catholicism) and emigrate to the US in the 1930s.

Adler was concerned with overcoming the superiority-inferiority dynamic and was one of the first psychotherapists to discard the analytic couch in favor of two chairs. The latter allows the clinician and patient to sit together more or less as equals. He was also an early feminist and holistic psychologist. Clinically, Adler's methods are not limited to treatment after-the-fact, but extend to the realm of prevention by preempting future problems in the child. Prevention strategies include encouraging and promoting social interest and belonging and a cultural shift within families and communities that leads to the eradication of both pampering and neglect. In other words, Adler stresses the social in psychology, unlike Freud.

His influence is vast. Much of Adler's work has been absorbed into modern psychology without attribution. Together with Freud and Jung, he is considered one of the fathers of depth psychology. He influenced the foremost founders of humanistic psychology, like Abraham Maslow, Rollo May, and so on. Instead of Freudian instinctual demands, in Adler's view individuals are fueled according to these figures by goals and an unknown creative force.

Frankl's school, then, is interested in the "will to meaning" which, for him, is more important than the pleasure principle on which Freud's psychoanalysis is founded or the "will to power" in Adlerian psychology. In his famous book *Man's Search for Meaning*, which is based on his experiences in the concentration camps, Frankl explores the psychological processes experienced by the prisoners. He observes that while all the functions of body and mind deteriorated or were reduced to the lowest common denominator, spiritual life continued. His recommendation for people undergoing extreme suffering is to remain brave, dignified, and unselfish in order to find a meaning and purpose. Further, he argues that dreaming and looking at suffering as if it is already in the past is helpful.

A prisoner who lost faith in the future loses hold of his inner self, Frankl writes. Whereas responsibility for another human being or for unfinished work keeps one alive. The meaning of life is infinite and suffering needs to be borne proudly. Frankl also describes the psychological reaction of prisoners after liberation. Freedom brings its own challenges and needs to be used wisely. People needed to be taught that they were not entitled to do wrong even if wrong had been done to them.

Frankl's "logotherapy" is based on discovering people's deep longings, on understanding love as grasping another human being in the innermost core of their personality, and sex as a vehicle for love. Suffering ceases to be suffering as soon as it finds a meaning.

It can thus be ennobling or degrading. Life lived to the fullest, even if it is transitory, is a source of satisfaction. Self-transcendence is the ultimate cure, whether through laughter, which causes self-detachment, or through walking away from obsessions by creating an opposite intention. An individual, Frankl believes, is essentially self-determining and can change at any moment. A person can lose their usefulness but not dignity. Thus, in the context of the Holocaust, Frankl believes that suffering can be turned into a human achievement and thereby transformed. It is the loss of an orientation towards meaning that causes death.

According to Frankl, thirty percent of the current population lacks meaning in life and lives in an existential vacuum—which leads to depression, aggression, and addiction. Yet meaning is available despite suffering and even through it. Value should be measured by dignity rather than usefulness. Love, work, pride in suffering, and personal growth are all sources of meaning. The challenge is to join the decent people in life, who are in a minority.

Frankl found a source of transformation, and his "exile" really leads back to the center of the individual, back to rejoining the human community. Unfortunately, not all of his co-prisoners had a chance or the capacity to do so. Frankl says in one of his studies that the meaning of man's life is connected with "the feeling that he lives for the sake of something or someone else."[65] During extreme and prolonged suffering, however, when a person is deprived of this "someone" or "something else, not everyone finds the strength to recreate these absences in their mind."[66] Frankl cautions that we tend to ascribe an absolute value to relative values. He says that despair has its roots in divinization, in the absolutization of some

---

[65] V. E. Frankl, "Das Gefühl, . . . für etwas, da zu sein—für etwas oder für jemand . . . ," in *Psychotherapie für den Layen. Rundfunkvorträge über Seelenheilkunde*, vol. 2 (Auflage, Freiburg im Breisgau: Herder, 1971), 50.

[66] Peter Tavel, "The Connection between Thomism and the Theory of Viktor E. Frankl on the Meaning and Goal of Life," *Angelicum* 87, no. 4 (2010): 867.

single relative value which, though significant, man regards as the only possible meaning of his life.

Frankl became one of the key figures of existential therapy and a prominent source of inspiration for humanistic psychologists. He lived in Vienna and often taught in the US; he received many honorary doctorates and prizes; he wrote thirty-nine books and was translated into forty languages. One of his great contributions also consists in stressing that freedom is only half of the story. The other half is responsibility.

Timothy Pytell, who offers an extensive historical background on Frankl's life and work, claims that Frankl actually spent only a few days in Auschwitz and yet "portrayed the Holocaust as a 'manageable' experience that (with luck) was survivable, but his version clashed with what we know about the 'reality' of Holocaust experience."[67] Frankl made survival in a concentration camp into a matter of mental health, and Lawrence Langer and Primo Levi have found his approach objectionable.

Timothy Pytell further documents both Frankl's semi-collaboration with the Nazis before and during WWII as well as his objectionable reconciliatory interaction with the Austrian Nazis in power following the war (for example, Kurt Waldheim). By accepting important awards from them, he helped legitimize their actions. Thus we have a very controversial figure before us—one who appealed to his American audience because he offered comfort with his claim that the Holocaust was basically a survivable trial and that anger should no longer be directed towards the Nazis. Furthermore, his well-known claim that there is "no collective guilt," that "there were good Nazis and bad Nazis," "good prisoners and bad prisoners" and, most significantly, "good SS and bad SS,"[68] helped to legitimize the Holocaust.

---

[67] Timothy Pytell, "The Missing Pieces of the Puzzle: A Reflection on the Odd Career of Viktor Frankl," *Journal of Contemporary History* 35, no. 2 (April 2000): 300.

[68] Speech given on Vienna Rathausplatz on March 10, 1988 on the fiftieth anniversary of "the occupation of Austria by the troops of Hitler's Germany."

As Pytell remarks, "Frankl was helping in the domestic rehabilitation of Waldheim. That Frankl took the medal from Waldheim in these circumstances (after the Waldheim affair) can only be construed as disgraceful."[69] However, Pytell also concedes that "this engagement in white-washing of the past was the only possibility in the post-war Austrian culture of denial and arguably Frankl's own choices in the 1930s colored his strategy for coming to terms with the past."[70] In America, on the other hand, he was a forerunner of the self-help movement and was widely recognized by spiritual psychologists who were seeking a way to reconcile the events of recent history with the existence of God and the possibility of a meaningful life too.

Reuven P. Bulka has, unlike Pytell, a very positive reading of Frankl. He believes that Frankl's logotherapy is a good response to the Holocaust, as it taught the world that positive meaning can be found in any situation. He argues that the Holocaust and Hitler gave the earth saints (like Frankl).[71] The ultimate question, from my point of view, then, is this: Is horror and misery acceptable if it proves that some individuals are capable of transcendence? Would it be preferable for people to live without the need for such heroism and instead enjoy a harmonious and peaceful world? Would it be better for the "weak" to have a decent life, not just the extremely strong or gifted?

Another, but very different, take on transcending death by transforming the world's consciousness can be found in the work of Simon Wiesenthal (b. 1908 in Buczacz/Buchach, Galicia, then part of Austria-Hungary, now Ternopil Oblast in Ukraine; d. 2005

---

[69]   Timothy Pytell, "The Missing Pieces of the Puzzle: A Reflection on the Odd Career of Viktor Frankl," *Journal of Contemporary History* 35, no. 2 (April 2000), 304.

[70]   Timothy Pytell, "Viktor Frankl: The Inside Outsider," in *Austrian Lives*, eds. Günter Bischof, Fritz Plasser, and Eva Maltschnig (New Orleans: University of New Orleans Press, 2012), 247.

[71]   Reuven P. Bulka, "Logotherapy as a Response to the Holocaust," *Tradition: A Journal of Orthodox Jewish Thought* 15, nos. 1/2 (Spring–Summer 1975): 89–96.

in Vienna). He lived in Lviv at the outbreak of WWII. Before that, however, he went to school in Vienna and studied at the Technical University in Prague, as Lviv University did not accept him due to his Jewishness. He miraculously survived six concentration camps — Janowska, Kraków-Płaszów, Gross-Rosen, Chemnitz, Buchenwald, and Mauthausen-Gusen. After the war, Wiesenthal dedicated his life to tracking down and gathering information on fugitive Nazi war criminals so that they could be brought to trial. Transforming the trauma of being an outcast in a strength, he sought justice for his murdered fellow citizens.

Wiesenthal was first an aide to the American War Crimes Office in Linz, where in 1947 he founded the Jewish Historical Documentation Center. There, he diligently collected information about Nazi criminals from Jewish camp survivors. The center was a one-man operation, which he financed with his own money; he lived very modestly, simply in gratitude for his incredible reunification with his wife and chance to have a regular family life. He even rejected any kind of German restitution payment, as he was not willing to accept German money in the wake of the brutal murder of eighty-nine members of his and his wife's family.

As Wiesenthal's agenda developed and his name became well known, he moved his operation to Vienna where in 1961 he opened the Documentation Center of the Association of Jewish Victims of the Nazi Regime. There, he continued the work of locating escaped Nazi criminals and helping Jews locate their displaced relatives. He was instrumental in high-profile cases, such as exposing the former Nazis in Bruno Kreisky government in 1970 and the Nazi past of the Austrian president and secretary general of the United Nations, Kurt Waldheim, in the 1980s.

This Ukrainian Jew became world famous for his untiring work on behalf of those who had no voice. Wiesenthal became the conscience of the world and deputy for the dead at a time when nobody wanted to hear about the horrors that the Jews suffered and at a time when antisemitism still prevailed in Europe. He only received occasional help from his fellow citizens and the relevant legal institutions often did not trust the information he provided. Even when he provided clear witnesses, they dragged out proceedings for years and the courts would dismiss the murderers on technicalities. There was really no hope that real justice could be achieved. Nevertheless, Wiesenthal succeeded in bringing to court some of the criminals who were protected by the new administration in Germany and, even more so, in Austria. These men had been helped by friendly and rich organizations like ODESSA (Organization der SS-Angehörigen), the Catholic Church in Italy, or non-extradition South American regimes. ODESSA, the secret escape organization of the SS underground, was especially effective in helping its members to escape justice. Another of Wiesenthal's achievements was the Austrian "Wiesenthal Law." It ruled that stolen works of art must be returned to their rightful owners.

His book *The Murderers Among Us* (1967) is a biographical, eye-opening account of some of his activities and experiences, his struggles and connections with the vast number of people who came to him for help. The book, consequently, is also an account of their lives. The stories collected in it are often unbelievable, yet every detail was painstakingly researched and verified. *The Murderers Among Us* reveals the lives of former inmates and victims of terror, as well as those of many important Nazi criminals—among them, Eichmann, Mengele, Bormann (Hitler's right hand), Stangl (the supervisor of the Hartheim Euthanasia Center and commander of Sobibor and Treblinka, who oversaw the death of about one million people), and Hermine Braunsteiner (the sadist at Majdanek and Ravensbruck).

Wiesenthal helped to locate some of these Nazis, such as Eichmann and Stangl, but he had to resign himself to many escaping for a variety of reasons. With so few witnesses left alive, the courts were obscenely lenient toward Nazi criminals. The struggle Wiesenthal undertook was truly heroic and awakened awe and admiration, not just for his courage and painstaking research, but for his unwavering sense of fairness and justice. He repeatedly overcame hurdles when trying to find Nazis who were protected by powerful institutions.

Wiesenthal shows that Austria was one of the worst nests of Nazism—war criminals could survive there long after the Third Reich was dead. It was the place where the Nazis had schooled themselves in technologies of mass murder by killing hundreds of thousands of their own compatriots first. These victims were called "lives not worthy of living."[72] A Galician himself, Wiesenthal explained why, later, most of the extermination camps were created in Poland and why the Jews of Ukraine suffered the worst. He pointed out that this was because in these countries the Germans were able to count on the help of the local population. These countries had no protective legislation to counteract the extermination law of the Nazis, and the level of antisemitism was disproportionately high compared to other parts of Central, Southern, and Western Europe where Jews were often protected by a sometimes substantial number of their fellow citizens.

The worst crimes were often kept secret from the population of the occupied countries. Not so in Galicia and Poland, where such crimes were often eagerly and sadistically carried out by the local population or with their full knowledge.[73] SS officers, Wiesenthal reports, were given the Cross of Merit (Kriegsverdienstkreuz) "for psychological discomfort" (*für seelische Belastung*—code for skill in the technique of mass extermination) due to working in such conditions.[74]

While he was born in one of the most unfortunate parts of the world at a most unfortunate time, Wiesenthal chose to emigrate to a hotbed of Nazis—Austria. It is true, they could not kill him or torture him anymore, but if he had wanted to live a peaceful life he could have gone to one of the English-speaking countries, where sympathy for the Nazis was almost nonexistent and where the legal system was not on the side of the criminals. In Austria, Nazis were able to hide easily and even obtain high administrative positions. They could even disappear without a trace.

The Cold War, which had set in by the 1950s, was also of help to the murderers. As long as they were willing to resist Communism,

---

[72] See introduction to Simon Wiesenthal, *The Murderers Among Us* (New York: McGraw-Hill Book Company, 1967).

[73] Ibid., 271.

[74] Ibid., 301.

Nazis could be incorporated into a country's political structure and even given high posts without any problems. After 1955, they were granted amnesty by various presidential decrees. Pending proceedings were suspended by the courts. Proven criminals were acquitted in Austria. Sometimes they were even applauded in the courtrooms.[75]

The history of Wiesenthal's hunts for Nazis is described in detail in a number of studies (see bibliography), particularly by Daniel Stahl, who confirms Wiesenthal's claims: "tracking down fugitives was not always the main problem in prosecuting Nazi criminals. Years of inactivity among investigative authorities, interpretations of laws that favored perpetrators and continued resistance to the idea of punishing Nazi crimes, greatly hindered efforts to pursue those who had gone underground in South America";[76] "Interpol's strict refusal to get involved in cases involving former Nazis doesn't fit in with the overall picture of the 1960s as a decade of manhunts for prominent fugitives";[77] "The Eichmann case had revealed how passively state and international institutions had acted and how much more needed to be done in hunting down Nazis."[78]

Wiesenthal's book brings together the individual stories of former camp inmates with his own biography against the backdrop of the politics of the period. It was written in the 1960s, twenty years after the crimes had been committed. The number of survivors was rapidly diminishing and their memories were already becoming less helpful in court. Indeed, until 1961, when the Israelis captured Eichmann in South America and tried him in Jerusalem, it was almost impossible to achieve any success or command any attention in Austria and Germany with regard to the issue. Those countries were simply in denial and were hoping that the past would simply

---

[75]   Ibid., 191.

[76]   Daniel Stahl, *Hunt for Nazis: South America's Dictatorships and the Prosecution of Nazi Crimes* (Amsterdam: Amsterdam University Press, 2018), 125–126.

[77]   Ibid., 153.

[78]   Ibid., 110.

disappear or be appeased by a few inane gestures. Wiesenthal was instrumental in making sure this did not happen and, in 1977, the Simon Wiesenthal Center, which continues his work, was created in Los Angeles.

In *The Murderers Among Us*, Wiesenthal has no truck with collective guilt:

> A Jew who believes in God and in his people, does not believe in the principle of collective guilt. Didn't Jews suffer for thousands of years because we were said to be collectively guilty—all of us, including the unborn children—of the crucifixion, the epidemics of the Middle Ages, communism, capitalism, bad wars, bad peace treaties? All ills of mankind, from the pestilence to the atomic bomb, are "the fault of the Jews." We are the eternal scapegoat. We know that we are not collectively guilty, so how can we accuse any other nation, no matter what some of its people have done, of being collectively guilty?[79]

The content of Wiesenthal's memoirs is so gripping that its form is practically see-through. Wiesenthal is an excellent narrator and his writing has an existential quality. He definitely transformed his own inner exile into a tireless fight for justice of the highest kind and is one of the best examples of giving life meaning. He sought justice for the dead, who could not thank him. He was resilient enough to perform this task for many decades and having lived a very long life. He succeeded in giving the Jewish dead a voice that could not be ignored and that contributed to the transformation of world awareness.

Wiesenthal has also left a powerful legacy in refusing to propose either resentment as an answer to the Holocaust (as Jean Améry did) or forgiveness of the perpetrators (as Eva Mozes Kor did). His answer is to raise the question of how to think through the Holocaust and leave the answer open. Peter Banki writes: "In what one might identify as a classical philosophical gesture, Wiesenthal interprets the demand for forgiveness of the Nazis and

---

[79]   Wiesenthal, *The Murderers Among Us*, 12.

their crimes *as a question*, which is to say, as an identifiable *topos* that can be situated and discussed as such."[80] He adds: "One can read *The Sunflower*[81] as the invention of a powerful resistance machine to the world's demand for closure and normalization."[82]

[80] Peter Banki, *The Forgiveness to Come: The Holocaust and the Hyper-Ethical* (New York: Fordham University Press, 2018), 44.

[81] Simon Wiesenthal, *The Sunflower: On the Possibilities and Limits of Forgiveness* (New York: Schocken Books, 1997).

[82] Ibid., 46.

Conclusion

This study has covered the various forms that exile took in the twentieth century by way of analyzing Jewish writers and thinkers (and occasionally other artists who address Jewish topics). I have chosen Jewish writers and thinkers because they exemplify ostracism's myriad effects and because the issue of exile was especially relevant to them in the period. Furthermore, the writing of Jewish exiles can be said to characterize the fate of modern man in general in recent times. Independent thinkers, creative individuals, and people who simply do not fit into the mainstream value system of the society in which they live have all experienced either literal exile (that is, leaving their home country) and/or have experienced the various forms of inner exile that I have delineated here.

The great wandering of Jews from Eastern Europe, particularly from the area of today's Ukraine, to Central and Western Europe, in order to escape pogroms or other abuses, eventually led many to leave for Palestine and create their own state, or just as often emigrate to America. Many outstanding Central European writers and scholars had successful careers and lived out their lives in the US. Some found temporary refuge in England or Sweden. This situation intensified, of course, with Hitler's coming to power and WWII, which ultimately lead to a large part of Europe falling under Soviet control. Oppressive regimes dominated the whole century, in fact.

The first part of the study (chapters 1 through 8) covers not only the forms of Jewish wandering, but the kinds of inner exile experienced in the first part of the twentieth century. It also explores the forms of behavior that reflected the decomposition of human values and that led to the later decimation of Jewish and human life—namely, the ban on different views and different varieties of artistic expression. These facts reflected themselves in the anxiety depicted by Freud and Kafka caused by the ever-increasing feeling of domination by oppressive institutions. The patriarchal way of life that we find in writers like Werfel or Ungar prophesied the cruel and inhuman ways of life to come. In both grotesque and subtle ways, their protagonists deal with discomfort—through murder and sexual abuse or through involuntary memory and the creation of dreamworlds. Finally, the marginalization of women and the image of the "femme fatale" was itself another part of the delinquent value system that characterized the twentieth century.

The second half of the book (chapters 9 through 15) covers the extreme forms of exile that followed in the wake of the Nazi concentration camps, where people were forced to face the inhumanity of their torturers and undergo dehumanization and a loss of identity. Many were simply put in the position of witnessing (Wiesel, Levi, Friedländer, Weiss). Witnessing, indeed, became one of the most important forms of exile after the Holocaust. But there were also other forms, such as new artistic, especially Surrealist, experiments (Fuks, Weil, Weiss) and an awakening of awareness that had been previously unknown. These writers exposed the emptiness of the mental world of the modern individual (see, in particular, Hostovský). The discovery of the pride and resistance that could be roused in certain radical situations was revolutionary. To an extent, some writers showed people that they could lose their fear of death (Lustig, Weil).

A new school of psychology was developed by Viktor Frankl, who based his claims on his experience of the death camps. He emphasized the need for meaning in human life and opposed earlier psychological schools that emphasized the pleasure and power principles as the main drivers of human behavior. This quest for meaning is profoundly and heroically exemplified in the work of Simon Wiesenthal, who devoted his whole life to securing justice for his destroyed brethren. In his writing, he poses the question of whether we can or should forgive the Nazis. Wisely, he gives no answer.

Exile thus ultimately shows itself as having a transformational power to bring us back to our essence and discover freedom. I refer to this in a personal essay mentioned in the introduction. Literal exile—which involves the loss of identity, nationhood, friends, culture, language, material possessions, communication, family, and in extreme cases a loss of life—strips authors of all their external characteristics and brings them to their fundamental human core. This is why mystic forms of expression are characteristic of exile poetry. We find such mysticism in twentieth-century Jewish poets such as Else Lasker-Schuller (Germany), Avram Sutzkever (Vilnius-Israel), Nelly Sachs (Germany-Sweden), Nina Cassian (Romania-US), Paul Celan (Romania-France), Jiří Orten (Czechoslovakia), Miklós Radnóti (Hungary), and others. Those that did not leave their country of origin during the crucial period discussed became outcasts and often perished. Their work should be the subject of another study.

As Eva C. Karpinski notes, in contemporary feminist writing on exile

> there has been a semantic shift among the meanings connoted by exile: what used to be associated with marginality and displacement is now more often linked to trans-nationality and nomadism. It shows that exile is no longer seen as a passive condition of being in the margin, being homeless, but it becomes a dynamic state suggesting movement across discursive and geographical spaces.[83]

External or literal exile is different from internal exile, of course. Internal exiles can enjoy their "home surroundings" and in that sense their exile is not as harsh. Our study, however, shows that internal and external exile are indeterminate concepts. Often, the internal exile in the twentieth century was the predecessor of the external exile. The conditions of internal exile brought their own challenges. Internal exile often ended in despair, imprisonment, or death. There is, however, a clear fluidity between the two kinds of exile which led to many forms of nomadic life during the period covered.

---

[83] Eva C. Karpinski, "Choosing Feminism, Choosing Exile: Towards the Development of a Transnational Feminist Consciousness," in *Emigré Feminism: Transnational Perspectives*, ed. Alena Heitlinger (Toronto: University of Toronto Press, 1999), 24.

Bibliography

Adorno, Theodor. *Minima Moralia: Reflections from Damaged Life.* Translated by E. F. N. Jephcott. London: New York: Verso, 1978 [1951].

Aleichem, Sholem. *Tevye's Daughters: Collected Stories of Sholom Aleichem.* NY: Crown, 1949 [1894].

Aleichem, Sholem, and Maurice Schwartz, dirs. *Tevye.* Magna Tech and International Cinema. 1939. Film.

Améry, Jean: *Bez viny a bez trestu: pokus o zvládnutí nezvládnutelného.* Translated by Daniela Petříčková and Miroslav Petříček. Praha: Prostor, 2011.

Anderson, Mark M. "The Child Victim as Witness to the Holocaust: An American Story?" *Jewish Social Studies* 14, no. 1 (Fall 2007): 1-22.

Arendt, Hannah. *Eichmann in Jerusalem: A Report on the Banality of Evil.* Harmondsworth: Penguin Books, 1984.

Banki, Peter. "The Survival of the Question: Simon Wiesenthal's The Sunflower," in *The Forgiveness to Come: The Holocaust and the Hyper-Ethical.* 20-48. New York: Fordham University Press, Modern Language Initiative, 2017.

Benvenga, Nancy. "Frankl, Newman and the Meaning of Suffering." *Journal of Religion and Health* 37, no. 1 (Spring 1998): 63-65.

Bílek, Petr. A. "Existencialismus v poválečné próze a poezii—tematika a kladení otázek." *Česká literatura* 51, no. 6 (December 2003): 735-737.

Biller, Karlheinz, Jay I. Levinson, and Timothy Pytell. "Viktor Frankl: Opposing Views." *Journal of Contemporary History* 37, no. 1 (January 2002): 105-113.

Broch, Hermann. *The Sleepwalkers.* New York: Vintage International; Random House, 1996.

———. *Hofmannsthal and His Time.* Chicago: The University of Chicago Press, 1984 [1948].

Brown, Wendy. "Tolerance as Museum Object: The Simon Wiesenthal Center Museum of Tolerance," in *Regulating Aversion: Tolerance in the Age of Identity and Empire,* 107-148. Princeton: Princeton University Press, 2006.

Bulka, Reuven P. "Logotherapy as a Response to the Holocaust." *Tradition: A Journal of Orthodox Jewish Thought* 15, nos. 1/2 (Spring-Summer 1975): 89-96.

Cedars, Marie M. Review of *Against Silence: The Voice and Vision of Elie Wiesel*, by Irwing Abrahamson. *Cross Currents* 36, no. 3 (Fall 1986): 257-266.

Celan, Paul. *Poems of Paul Celan: A Bilingual German/English Edition.* Translated by Michael Hamburger. Rev. ed. New York: Persea, 2002.

Cohen, Robert. "The Political Aesthetics of Holocaust Literature: Peter Weiss's *The Investigation* and Its Critics." *History and Memory* 10, no. 2 (Fall 1998): 43-67.

Davidheiser, James C. "The Novelist as Prophet: A New Look at Franz Werfel's "Höret die Stimme." *Modern Austrian Literature* 24, no. 2 (1991): 51-67.

Demetz, Peter. "Kafka, Freud, Husserl: Probleme einer Generation," *Zeitschrift fürReligions—und Geistesgeschichte* 7, no. 1 (1955): 59-69.

Despard, Lucy. Review of *Justice Not Vengeance*, by Simon Wiesenthal. *Foreign Affairs* 69, no. 3 (Summer 1990): 182.

Diamond, Denis. "Elie Wiesel: Reconciling the Irreconcilable." *World Literature Today* 57, no. 2 (Spring 1983): 228-233.

Drubek-Meyer, Natascha. "Opfer und 'Leichenverbrenner' Das 'jüdische Thema' in tschechischer Literatur und Film," *Osteuropa* 58, no. 6 (June 2008): 341-356.

Ezrahi, Sidra DeKoven. *Booking Passage: Exile and Homecoming in the Modern Jewish Imagination.* Berkeley: University of California Press, 2000.

Farrell, Joseph. "The Humanity and Humanism of Primo Levi'" In *Answering Auschwitz: Primo Levi's Science and Humanism after the Fall*, edited by Stanislao G. Pugliese, 87-102. New York: Fordham University Press, 2011.

Frankl, Viktor. "Facing the Transitoriness of Human Existence." *Journal of the American Society on Aging* 14, no. 4 (Fall 1990): 7-10.

———. *Man's Search for Meaning.* Boston: Beacon Press, 1992 [1946; first English edition 1959].

———. *Psychotherapie für den Layen. Rundfunkvorträge über Seelenheilkunde.* Vol. 2. Auflage, Freiburg im Breisgau: Herder, 1971.

Frederick, John T. "Franz Werfel and "The Song of Bernadette." *The English Journal* 32, no. 3 (March 1943): 119-125.

Freud, Sigmund. *The Future of an Illusion*. Translated by James Strachey. New York: Norton, 1989 [1927].

Friedländer, Saul. *Nazi Germany and the Jews, 1939–1945: The Years of Extermination*. New York: Harper Collins Publishers, 2007.

– – –. *When Memory Comes: The Classic Memoir*. Translated by Helen R. Lane. New York: Farrar, Straus and Giroux, 1979 [1978].

Garloff, Katja. *Words from Abroad: Trauma and Displacement in Postwar German Jewish Writers*. Detroit: Wayne State UP, 2005.

George, Diana. Review of *Boys & Murderers: Collected Short Fiction*, by Hermann Ungar. *Chicago Review* 53, no. 2/3 (Autumn 2007): 206-208.

Gerstenfeld, Manfred. "The Multiple Distortions of Holocaust memory." *Jewish Political Studies Review* 19, no. 3/4 (Fall 2007): 35-55.

Giroud, Françoise. *Alma Mahler or the Art of Being Loved*. Oxford: Oxford UP, 1991.Goldhaber, Michael D. *A People's History of the European Court of Human Rights*. New Jersey: Rutgers University Press, 2007.

Goldstein, Yossi. "Eastern Jews vs. Western Jews: The Ahad Ha'am-Herzl Dispute and Its Cultural and Social Implications." *Jewish History* 24, nos. 3/4 (2010): 355-377.

Hales, Barbara. "Projecting Trauma: The Femme Fatale in Weimar and Hollywood Film Noir." *Women in German Yearbook* 23 (2007): 224-243.

Haman, Aleš. *Arnošt Lustig*. Prague: H & H, 1995.

Harrowitz, Nancy. *Primo Levi and the Identity of a Survivor*. Toronto: University of Toronto Press, 2017.

Heim, Michael. "Egon Hostovský by Rudolf Šturm." *Books Abroad* 49, no. 2 (Spring 1975): 353.

Heitlinger, Alena, ed. *Émigré Feminism. Transnational Perspectives*. Toronto: University of Toronto Press, 1999.

Heitlingerová, Alena. *Ve stínu holocaustu a komunismu (Čeští a slovenští židé po roce 1945)*. Prague: G+G, 2007.

Herzl, Theodor. *The Jewish State*. Translated by Sylvie d'Avigdor, New York: Dover Publications, 1988 [1895].

Hikl, Mario. "Czechoslovak Literature in Exile." *Slavic and East-European Studies* 7, nos. 1/2 (Spring–Summer 1962): 102-107.

Hirsch, Marianne, "Past Lives." In *Exile and Creativity: Signposts, Travelers, Outsiders, Backward Glances*, edited by Rubin Suleiman. Durham: Duke University Press, 1998, 418-446.

von Hofmannsthal, Hugo. *The Tower*. In *Selected Plays and Libretti*. Translated by Various. New York: Bolingen Foundation, 1963 [1925], 173-378.

Holý, Jiří. "'Shoah' als Thema in der polnischen, tschechischen und slowakischen Literatur." *Zeitschrift für Slavische Philologie* 63, no. 2 (2004): 363-375.

———. "Subjektivizované vyprávění v er-formě." *Česká literatura* 49, no. 3 (2001): 227-242.

———. "Židé, antisemitský diskurz a dvojí zpracování tématu šoa ve střední Evropě." *Česká literatura* 59, no. 6 (December 2011): 887-895.

———. "Znovunalezené dětství—Nezval, Schulz, Hostovský." *Česká literatura* 46, no. 1 (1998): 3-14.

Hostovský, Egon. *The Midnight Patient*. Translated by Philip Hillyer Smith, Jr. London: Heinemann, 1955.

———.*Všeobecné spiknutí*, Prague: Melantrich, 1969.

Israel, Nico. *Outlandish*. Stanford: Stanford UP, 2000.

Kafka, Franz. *Amerika.* Translated by Mark Harman. New York: Schocken Books, 2008 [1927].

———. *The Penal Colony: Stories and Short Pieces*. Translated by Edwin and Willa Muir. New York: Schocken Books, 1948 [1919].

Karpowitz, Stephen."The Dilemma of Primo Levi—Biographical Roots." *European Judaism: A Journal for the New Europe* 28, no. 2 (Autumn 1995): 61-67.

Kautman, František. *Polarita našeho věku v díle Egona Hostovského*. Prague: Evropský kulturní klub, 1993.

Kettler, David and Zvi Ben-Dor. "Introduction: The Limits of Exile." *Journal of the Interdisciplinary Crossroads* 3, no. 1 (2006): 1-9.

Kieval, Hillel J. "Choosing to Bridge: Revisiting the Phenomenon of Cultural Mediation." *Bohemia Band* 46 (2005): 15-27.

Knapp, Bettina Liebowitz. *Exile and Writer: Exoteric and Esoteric Experiences*. Pennsylvania: Pennsylvania State University Press, 1991.

Kowalik, Jill Anne. "Attachment, Patriarchal Anxiety, and Paradigm Selection in German Literary Criticism." *The German Quarterly* 77, no. 1 (Winter 2004): 1-8.

Kraus, Karl. *The Last Days of Mankind*. Translated by Various. New York: Frederick Ungar Publishing, 1974 [1919].

Kundera, Milan. "Kafka's World." *The Wilson Quarterly* 12, no. 5 (Winter 1988): 88–99.

von Kunes, Karen. "Indecent Dreams by Arnošt Lustig." *World Literature Today* 63, no. 250 (Spring 1989): 331.

Langer, Lawrence L. *The Holocaust and the Literary Imagination.* New Haven: Yale University Press, 1975.

Lantz, Jim. "Art, Logotherapy, and the Unconscious God." *Journal of Religion and Health* 32, no. 3 (Fall 1993): 179-187.

Lederbuchová, Ladislava. "Ladislav Fuks a literární mystifikace." *Česká literatura* 34, no. 3 (1986): 234-244.

Levi, Primo. *If This is a Man.* Translated by Stuart Woolf. New York: Orion Press, 1959 [1947].

— — —. *The Drowned and the Saved.* Translated from the Italian by Raymond Rosenthal. New York: Summit Books (Simon & Schuster), 1988.

— — —. *The Truce: A Survivor's Journey Home from Auschwitz.* Translated by Stuart Woolf. London: Folio Society, 2002 [1965].

Liehm, A. J. "Egon Hostovský: A Last Conversation." *Canadian Slavonic Papers* 16, no. 4 (Winter 1974): 539-568.

Lisus, Nicola A. and Richard V. Ericson. "Misplacing Memory: The Effect of Television Format on Holocaust Remembrance." *The British Journal of Sociology* 46, no. 1 (March 1995): 1-19.

Lower, Wendy. *German Women in the Nazi Killing Fields.* Boston: Houghton Mifflin Harcourt, 2013.

Lustig, Arnošt. *Démanty noci* (Diamonds of the Night). Prague: Hynek, 1998.

— — —. *Dita Saxova.* Toronto: 68 Publishers, 1982.

— — —. *Modlitba pro Kateřinu Horowitzovou (Prayer for Katarina Horowitzova).* Prague: Československý spisovatel, 1967.

— — —. *Nemilovaná* (Unloved). Prague: Odeon, 1991.

Manseau, Peter. "Revising Night: Elie Wiesel and the Hazards of Holocaust Theology." *Cross Currents* 56, no. 3 (Fall 2006): 387-399.

McClellan, William. "Primo Levi and the History of Reception." In *Answering Auschwitz: Primo Levi's Science and Humanism after the Fall,* edited by Stanislao G. Pugliese. New York: Fordham University Press, 2011: 41-55.

Meissner, Frank. "German Jews of Prague: A Quest for Self-Realization." *Publications of the American Jewish Historical Society* 50, no. 2 (December 1960): 98-120.

Merhaut, Luboš. "Nelehká cesta za poznáním zla (Interpretace Fuksova románu Myši Natálie Mooshabrové)." *Česká literatura* 37, no. 5 (1989): 398-412.

Musil, Robert. *The Man without Qualities.* Translated by Sophie Wilkins. New York: Alfred A. Knopf, 1995 [1932].

Nordau, Max. *The Conventional Lies of Our Civilization.* Chicago: L. Schick, 1887 [1883].

———. *Degeneration.* Translated by Howard Fertig. New York: Howard Fertig, 1968 [1892].

Oren, Michael. "The Many Holocausts." *The Atlantic,* January 26, 2020.

Papoušek, Vladimír. "Egon Hostovský a Lewis Mumford." *Česká literatura* 43, no. 5 (1995): 510-518.

Papoušek, Vladimír. *Egon Hostovský: člověk v uzavřeném prostoru,* Prague: H&H, 1996.

———. *Trojí samota ve velké zemi (Česká literatura v americkém exilu v letech 1938–1968).* Prague: H & H, 2001.

Peck, Clemens. "Theodor Herzl and the Utopia of the Salon in Fin-de-Siècle Vienna." *Austrian Studies* 24 (2016): 79-93.

Pynsent, Robert. *Decadence and Innovation: Austro-Hungarian life and Art at the Turn of the Century.* London: Weidenfeld and Nicolson, 1989.

Pytell, Timothy. "The Missing Pieces of the Puzzle: A Reflection on the Odd Career of Viktor Frankl." *Journal of Contemporary History* 35, no. 2 (April 2000): 281-306.

———. "Viktor Frankl: The Inside Outsider." In *Austrian Lives,* edited by Günter Bischof, Fritz Plasser, and Eva Maltschnig, 240-255. New Orleans: University of New Orleans Press, 2012.

Rosenbaum, Ron. "Elie Wiesel's Secret." *Tablet,* September 29, 2017.

Rosenfeld, Alvin H. "The Assault on Holocaust Memory." *KulturPoetik* 2, no. 1 (2002): 82-101.

———. *A Double Dying: Reflections on Holocaust Literature.* Bloomington: Indiana University Press, 1980.

Roth, Joseph. *The Wandering Jews: Essays.* Translated by Michael Hoffmann. New York-London: W. W. Norton, 2001 [1926].

Rothberg, Abraham. Review of *A Prayer for Katerina Horovitzova*, by Arnost Lustig. *Southwest Review* 59, no. 1 (Winter 1974): 87-89.

Rothberg, Michael and Jonathan Druker. "A Secular Alternative: Primo Levi's Place in American Holocaust Discourse." *Shofar* 28, no. 1 (Fall 2009): 104-126.

Rubin Suleiman, Susan. *Exile and Creativity: Signposts, Travelers, Outsiders, Backward Glances.* Durham and London: Duke University Press, 1998.

Said, Edward. *Reflections on Exile.* Cambridge, MA: Harvard UP, 2000.

———. *Representations of the Intellectual.* New York: Pantheon Books, 1994.

Schlein, Rena A. "The Motif of Hypocrisy in the Works of Arthur Schnitzler." *Modern Austrian Literature* 2, no. 1 (Spring 1969): 28-38.

Schlunk, Jürgen E. "Auschwitz and Its Function in Peter Weiss' Search for Identity." *German Studies Review* 10, no. 1 (February 1987): 11-30.

Schnitzler, Arthur. *Professor Bernhardi.* Translated by Hetty Landstone. New York: Simon & Schuster, 1928 [1913].

Schubert, Peter Z. "The Unloved: From the Diary of Perla S by Arnošt Lustig." Translated by Vera Kalina-Levine." *World Literature Today* 60, no. 4 (Autumn 1986): 655.

Schulz, Bruno. *The Street of Crocodiles.* Translated by Celina Wieniewska. New York: Walker and Company, 1963 [1957].

Seidman, Naomi. "Elie Wiesel and the Scandal of Jewish Rage." *Jewish Social Studies* 3, no. 1 (Autumn 1996): 1-19.

Shore, Marci. "From *Tanga, a Girl from Hamburg* by Arnošt Lustig." *The Kenyon Review* 24, no. 2 (Spring 2002): 65-75.

Sokel, Walter H. "The Other Face of Expressionism." *Monatshefte* 47, no. 1 (January 1955): 1-10.

Spitzer, Leo, "Persistent Memory." In Rubin Suleiman, *Exile and Creativity.*

Stahl, Daniel. *Hunt for Nazis: South America's Dictatorships and the Prosecution of Nazi Crimes.* Amsterdam: Amsterdam University Press, 2018.

Štědroňová, Eva. "Dialektika umělecké metody a reality v díle Jiřího Weila." *Česká literatura* 38, no. 2 (1990): 126-140.

Štěpař, Vaclav. "Odraz židovského útlaku za 2. sv. války u nás v dílech českých spisovatelů 20. st." PhD diss., Technická univerzita v Liberci, 2008.

Stephan, Alexander, ed. *Exile and Otherness: New Approaches to the Experience of the Nazi Refugees*. Oxford: Peter Lang, 2005.

Stier, Oren Baruch. "Virtual Memories: Mediating the Holocaust at the Simon Wiesenthal Center's Beit Hashoah-Museum of Tolerance." *Journal of the American Academy of Religion* 64, no. 4 (Winter 1996): 831-851.

Strelka, Joseph. "Probleme der Erforschung der deutschsprachigen Exilliteratur seit 1933." *Colloquia Germanica* 10, no. 2 (1976/1977): 140-153.

Šturm, Rudolf, ed. *Egon Hostovský*, Toronto: 68 Publishers, 1974.

———. "Všeobecné spiknutí by Egon Hostovský." *Books Abroad* 45, no. 1 (Winter 1971): 145.

Sundquist, Eric J. "Witness without End?" *American Literary History* 19, no. 1 (Spring 2007): 65-85.

Tavel, Peter. "The Connection between Thomism and the Theory of Viktor E. Frankl on the Meaning and Goal of Life," *Angelicum* 87, no. 4 (2010): 861-869.

Timms, Edward. *Karl Kraus, Apocalyptic Satirist: Culture and Catastrophe in Habsburg Vienna*. New Haven: Yale UP, 1986.

Todorov, Tzvetan. "Ten Years Without Primo Levi." *Salmagundi*, nos. 116/117 (Fall/Winter 1997): 3-18.

Townsend, Charles E. "Dita Saxova by Arnošt Lustig." *Slavic Review* 54, no. 2 (Summer 1995): 458-459.

Ungar, Hermann. *Boys & Murderers: Collected Short Fiction*. Prague, Twisted Spoon Press, 2006 [1920].

———. *The Maimed*. Prague: Twisted Spoon Press, 2002 [1922].

Urzidil, Johannes. *There Goes Kafka*. Detroit: Wayne State UP, 1968.

Vaněk, Václav. "Vedlejší postavy v románech Egona Hostovského." *Česká literatura* 39, no. 6 (1991): 526-538.

Vicinus, Martha. "The Adolescent Boy: Fin de Siècle Femme Fatale?" *Journal of the History of Sexuality* 5, no. 1 (July 1994): 90-114.

Volková, Bronislava. "Exil: psychologický, kulturně-historický, duchovní." *Český Dialog* 5 (2015).

———. "Exil vnitřní a vnější." *Listopad* (2004): 12-19.

— — —. "Exile: Inside and Out." In *The Writer Uprooted: Contemporary Jewish Exile Literature)*, edited Alvin H. Rosenfeld, 161-176. Bloomington: Indiana UP, 2008.

— — —. "Psychological, Cultural, Historical and Spiritual Aspects of Exile." *Comenius, Journal of Euro-American Civilization* 1, no 2 (2014): 199-212.

Wagener, Hans. "Winning the Jackpot: German Exile Writers Who Made It Big." *Pacific Coast Philology* 27, nos. 1/2 (September 1992): 3-9.

Walker, Heidi Ann, and Elie Wiesel. "Why and How I Write: An Interview with Elie Wiesel." *The Journal of Education* 162, no.2 (Spring 1980): 57-63.

Wassel, Adam M. "Perpetrator Parables: Simon Wiesenthal's 'The Sunflower' and Joseph Conrad's 'Heart of Darkness.'" *CEA Critic* 76, no. 3 (November 2014): 232-238.

Weil, Jiří. *Life with a Star.* New York: Farrar Straus & Giroux, 1989 (1949).

Weininger, Otto. *Sex and Character.* London and New York: G. P. Putnam's Sons, 1906.

Weiss, Peter. *The Investigation.* Translated by Jon Swan and Ulu Grosbard. New York: Atheneum, 1966 [1965].

Weiskopf, F. C. "*Listy z vyhnanství* (Letters from Exile) by Egon Hostovsky." *Books Abroad* 15, no. 4 (Autumn 1941): 467

— — —. "Cizinec hledá byt by Egon Hostovský." *Books Abroad* 21, no. 4 (Autumn 1947): 418.

Wellek, René. "Hofmannsthal's World." *The New Criterion* 4, no. 4 (1985): 75.

Werfel, Franz. *The Forty Days of Musa Dagh.* Translated by Geoffrey Dunlop. New York: Modern Library, 1934.

— — —. *Hearken onto the Voice.* Translated by Moray Firth. New York: Viking, 1938.

— — —. *Jacobowsky and the Colonel.* Translated by S. N. Behrman. New York: Random House, 1944.

— — —. "Not the Murderer." In *Twilight of a World.* Translated by H. T. Lowe-Porter. New York: The Viking Press, 1937 [1919], 567-692.

— — —. *The Song of Bernadette.* Translated by Luwig Lewisohn New York: The Viking Press, 1942.

Wiesel, Elie. *Night*. Translated by Marion Wiesel. New York: Hill and Wang, 2006 [1958].

Wiesenthal, Simon. *The Murderers Among Us*. Edited by Joseph Wechsberg. New York: McGraw-Hill Book Company, 1967.

———. *The Sunflower: On the Possibilities and Limits of Forgiveness*. New York: Schocken Books, 1997.

Wistrich, Robert S. "Karl Kraus: Jewish Prophet or Renegade?" *European Judaism: A Journal for the New Europe* 9, no.2 (Summer 1975): 32-38.

Wohlfarth, Irwing. "Manner aus der Fremde": Walter Benjamin and the "German-Jewish Parnassus." *New German Critique*, no. 70 (Winter 1997): 3-85.

Zilbersheid, Uri. "The Utopia of Theodor Herzl." *Israel Studies* 9, no. 2 (Fall 2004): 80-114.

Zolkos, Magdalena, ed. *On Jean Améry: Philosophy of Catastrophe*. New York: Lexington Books, 2011.

Zuroff, Efraim. "Eastern Europe: Antisemitism in the Wake of Holocaust-Related Issues." *Jewish Political Studies Review* 17, nos. 1/2 (Spring 2005): 63-79.

———. "Sweden's Refusal to Prosecute Nazi War Criminals — 1986-2002." *Jewish Political Studies Review* 14, nos. 3/4 (Fall 2002): 85-117.

Zweig, Stefan. *The World of Yesterday*. Translated by Anthea Bell. Lincoln: University of Nebraska Press, 1964 [1943].

Index

CPSIA information can be obtained
at www.ICGtesting.com
Printed in the USA
JSHW042000140621
15887JS00003B/156

9 781644 695906